D0684678

Stand

A Call for the Endurance of the Saints

John Piper | Justin Taylor

GENERAL EDITORS

CROSSWAY BOOKS

WHEATON, ILLINOIS

Stand

Copyright © 2008 by Desiring God

Published by Crossway Books
    a publishing ministry of Good News Publishers
    1300 Crescent Street
    Wheaton, Illinois 60187

All rights reserved. No part of this publication may be reproduced, stored in a retrieval system or transmitted in any form by any means, electronic, mechanical, photocopy, recording or otherwise, without the prior permission of the publisher, except as provided for by USA copyright law.

Cover design: Matthew Taylor

Cover photo: Getty Images

First printing, 2008

Printed in the United States of America

Unless otherwise indicated, Scripture quotations are taken from *The Holy Bible: English Standard Version®*. Copyright © 2001 by Crossway Bibles, a publishing ministry of Good News Publishers. Used by permission. All rights reserved.

Scripture references marked NIV are from *The Holy Bible: New International Version®*. Copyright © 1973, 1978, 1984 by International Bible Society. Used by permission of Zondervan Publishing House. All rights reserved. The "NIV" and "New International Version" trademarks are registered in the United States Patent and Trademark Office by International Bible Society. Use of either trademark requires the permission of International Bible Society.

Scripture references marked NASB are from *The New American Standard Bible®*. Copyright © The Lockman Foundation 1960, 1962, 1963, 1968, 1971, 1972, 1973, 1975, 1977, 1995. Used by permission.

Scripture references marked KJV are from *The Holy Bible: King James Version*.

Scripture references marked NKJV are from *The Holy Bible: New King James Version*. Copyright © 1982, Thomas Nelson, Inc. Used by permission.

All emphases in Scripture quotations have been added by the authors.

PDF ISBN: 978-1-4335-0476-1

Mobipocket ISBN: 978-1-4335-0477-8

Library of Congress Cataloging-in-Publication Data
Stand : a call for the endurance of the saints / John Piper and
Justin Taylor, general editors.
   p. cm.
   Includes bibliographical references and indexes.
   ISBN 978-1-4335-0114-2 (tpb)
   1. Perseverance (Theology) I. Piper, John, 1946–   . II. Taylor, Justin,
1976–   . III. Title.
BT768.S73   2008
243—dc22   2008008297

ML		17	16	15	14	13	12	11	10	09	08
15	14	13	12	11	10	9	8	7	6	5	4	3	2	1

To
JOHN MACARTHUR

*whose life and ministry stands
on the Word of God*

Contents

Contributors

Randy Alcorn is the founder and director of Eternal Perspective Ministries (EPM). Before founding EPM in 1990, he served as a pastor for fourteen years. He has spoken around the world and has taught on the adjunct faculties of Multnomah Bible College and Western Seminary in Portland, Oregon. Randy is the best-selling author of twenty-seven books including the novels *Safely Home* and *Deception*. His fourteen nonfiction works include *Money, Possessions, and Eternity*; *The Treasure Principle*; *The Purity Principle*; *The Grace and Truth Paradox*; *Why ProLife?* and *Heaven*. Randy has written for many magazines and produces the popular periodical *Eternal Perspectives*. The father of two married daughters, Randy lives in Gresham, Oregon, with his wife and best friend, Nanci.

Jerry Bridges is a well-known Christian writer and conference speaker whose best-known book, *The Pursuit of Holiness*, has sold well over a million copies. His nine published books have sold over 2.5 million copies and have been translated and published in sixteen different languages. In addition to his writing ministry, Jerry also serves as a guest lecturer at several seminaries and speaks at numerous conferences all over the world. He has served on the staff of The Navigators since 1955 and currently serves as a resource person to The Navigators University Students Ministry in the United States. Jerry received an honorary doctor of divinity degree from Westminster Theological Seminary. He and his wife, Jane, have two married children and six grandchildren and reside in Colorado Springs.

John MacArthur is a popular author and conference speaker and has served as pastor-teacher of Grace Community Church in Sun Valley, California, since 1969. John is a fifth-generation pastor, and his pulpit ministry has been extended around the globe through his media ministry, Grace to You, and its satellite offices in Australia, Canada, Europe, India, New Zealand, Singapore, and South Africa. In addition to producing daily radio programs for nearly two thousand English and Spanish radio outlets worldwide, Grace to You distributes his books, software, audiotapes, and CDs. In thirty-six years of ministry, Grace to You has distributed more than thirteen million CDs and audiotapes. John is the president of The Master's College and The Master's Seminary, and he has written hundreds of books and study guides. His best-selling titles include *The Gospel According to Jesus*; *Ashamed of the Gospel*; *Twelve Ordinary Men*; and *The MacArthur Study Bible*, a 1998 ECPA Gold Medallion recipient. John and his wife, Patricia, have four grown children and fourteen grandchildren.

John Piper is pastor for preaching and vision at Bethlehem Baptist Church in Minneapolis. He grew up in Greenville, South Carolina, and studied at Wheaton College, where he first sensed God's call to enter the ministry. He went on to earn degrees from Fuller Theological Seminary (BD) and the University of Munich (DTheol). For six years he taught Biblical Studies at Bethel College in Saint Paul, Minnesota, and in 1980 accepted the call to serve as pastor of Bethlehem Baptist Church. He has written, among other books, *Desiring God*; *Don't Waste Your Life*; *God Is the Gospel*; *Battling Unbelief*; and *What Jesus Demands from the World*. He is married to Noël and has four sons, one daughter, and eight grandchildren.

Helen Roseveare was born in England in 1925. She was born again while a medical student at Cambridge University in 1945, joined WEC International missionary society in 1950, and sailed for the Belgian Congo in 1953. Helen served first under Belgian colonial rule, then during the transfer to independence, then through the civil war in 1965, and finally in what became Zaire (renamed the Democratic Republic of Congo). During the next twenty years, Helen ministered by setting up a rural hospital, several rural clinics, and a training school for national paramedical workers, and by joining in the formation of a large inter-mission referral hospital and training college for nurses and midwives. Since 1973 she has served on the home-end of WEC International as a deputation worker, speaking to young people, university students, and church groups all over the English-speaking world, challenging them to consider God's claim on their lives for full-time service. She has also written several books for her mission, underlining principles for Christian living and missionary outreach work.

Justin Taylor is the project director and managing editor of the ESV Study Bible (2008) and an associate publisher at Crossway Books. With Kelly Kapic he has edited new editions of two classic works by John Owen: *Overcoming Sin and Temptation* and *Communion with the Triune God*. And with John Piper he has edited a number of books from the Desiring God conferences: *A God-Entranced Vision of All Things*; *Sex and the Supremacy of Christ*; *Suffering and the Sovereignty of God*; and *The Supremacy of Christ in a Postmodern World*. He blogs daily at Between Two Worlds (http://theologica.blogspot.com/). He and his wife, Lea, have three children.

Introduction

Justin Taylor

John Piper recently recounted his father's unwavering faith, even in his closing years:

> Even in his final years of dementia, he rejoiced. In the last month that he was able to keep a journal (April of 2004), he wrote, "I'll soon be 86 but I feel strong and my health is good. God has been exceedingly gracious and I am most unworthy of His matchless grace and patience. *The Lord is more precious to me the older I get.*"[1]

Read that final line again, slowly. What an amazing sentence—even in the midst of dementia, he felt the increasing preciousness of the presence of Christ. One of the purposes of the book you hold in your hands is to encourage you and equip you to truthfully write such a sentence—and mean it—in the final season of your life.

What Is Perseverance and Endurance?

One of the best biblical definitions concerning the path of endurance and perseverance is provided in the apostle Paul's statement, "Not that I have already obtained this or am already perfect, but I press on to make it my own, because Christ Jesus has made me his own" (Phil. 3:12). Beginning at the end, we can note three truths he taught here: first, the foundation of Paul's (and our) perseverance is that Christ has made us his own. Jesus says to us what he said to his disciples: "You did not choose me, but I chose you . . ." (John 15:16). Christ is the initiator in this relationship. Second, we have not yet arrived. There is no ultimate arrival—either qualitatively or temporally—prior to

---

[1] John Piper, "Evangelist Bill Piper: Fundamentalist Full of Grace and Joy," delivered at the Desiring God Pastors Conference (February 5, 2008); emphasis added. Available at www.desiringGod.org.

standing face-to-face with God himself. We are in process, still in the midst of the fight, still running the race. God "began a good work" in us, but he will only "bring it to completion at the day of Jesus Christ" (Phil. 1:6). Finally, despite the fact that it is ultimately God's work, it is done *through* our work, not *instead* of our work. Paul says that we must "press on," making it our own.

Building off of such teaching, theologian John Murray proposed a definition to take account of the full biblical witness on this theme: "Perseverance means the engagement of our persons in the most intense and concentrated devotion to those means which God has ordained for the achievement of his saving purpose."[2] Note a number of things: first, perseverance involves not just a part of us (mind or body or spirit), but all of us—our whole person. Second, it involves "the most intense and concentrated devotion." No one should drift toward the finish line. It involves serious effort (which is why Paul compared it to a fight and a race!). Third, intense, whole-person devotion is only as good as its object. Therefore Murray makes clear that the devotion must be to "those means which God has ordained for the achievement of his saving purpose." God's people will persevere by God's grace by using God's means ("especially the Word, sacraments, and prayer"[3]) to the advancement of God's glory.

Overview of the Contributors

In accordance with Philippians 3:12, none of the contributors to this book will claim to have already obtained full sanctification; but each of them is pressing on to make it his or her own because Christ Jesus has first made them his own.

You'll notice that each contributor has decades of experience in walking with Jesus. Helen Roseveare was born in 1925, Jerry Bridges in 1928, John MacArthur in 1939, John Piper in 1946. Randy Alcorn is the youngster of the group, born in 1954.

As someone a few years younger than these wise saints, I think it would be a grave mistake to assume that this is therefore a book only for those who are older. All Christians, no matter their age, want to

---

[2]John Murray, *Redemption—Accomplished and Applied* (Grand Rapids, MI: Eerdmans, 1955), 192–193.
[3]Westminster Larger Catechism, Answer #154.

make it to the end. And we don't want to barely make it by the skin of our teeth, but to "lay aside every weight, and sin which clings so closely, and . . . run with endurance the race that is set before us, looking to Jesus, the founder and perfecter of our faith" (Heb. 12:1–2). One of the best ways we can do this is to sit at the feet of those who have spent years running with Jesus.

Overview of the Chapters

Jerry Bridges says there are four foundational, fundamental actions that will enable us to fight the good fight of faith and to finish well: (1) a daily time of focused personal communion with God; (2) a daily appropriation of the gospel; (3) a daily commitment to be a living sacrifice to God; (4) a firm belief in the sovereignty and love of God. Bridges reminds us that our aim is not only to persevere but to endure—not only to stand firm but to move forward toward the finish line and the presence of God in glory.

John Piper addresses the question of how to get old to the glory of God. The key, he says, is to grow old in a way that makes God (and not the world) look glorious and all-satisfying. But a significant obstacle toward this goal is the fear of not maintaining a treasuring of Christ. Two common strategies seek to overcome this fear: (1) the belief that perseverance in faith and love are not essential for final salvation, and (2) the belief that the necessity of perseverance depends on our own efforts. Piper explains why both views are dead wrong: perseverance is necessary for final salvation, and perseverance is certain for all those who are in Christ. The biblical antidote for overcoming the fear of not preserving is to see the fight of faith as a fight to delight in Christ as our highest treasure.

John MacArthur has been in pastoral ministry at one church long enough to witness every kind of attack imaginable: on his character, his life, and his ministry. So in order to learn how to survive, MacArthur has made a lifelong study of Paul's life. Drawing especially upon a careful examination of 2 Corinthians, MacArthur shows what Paul embraced:

- the superiority of the new covenant
- the reality that ministry is a mercy
- the necessity of a pure heart

- the duty of accurately handling the Word of God
- the truth that the results of his ministry did not depend on him
- the reality of his own insignificance
- the benefits of suffering
- the need for bold conviction
- eternity as the priority

Randy Alcorn, at our request, recounts his own family's persever-ance in a trial. He also explains some of the things he has learned from endurance in a cause: namely, that we should be motivated by Jesus, not by anger; that endurance in a cause can build the character, faith, and insight of children; and that followers of Jesus should expect injustice and misrepresentation. With regard to endurance in general, Alcorn observes that who you become is the product of the daily choices you make—what you daily choose to delight in and meditate upon. Alcorn closes by telling the moving story of Jim Elliot's brother, the one whom almost no one knows.

Helen Roseveare has lived a fascinating life of endurance with Christ. In her personal and biblical chapter, she touches upon the past, the present, and the future testimony of her Christian life, orga-nized around the theme of "one thing." First, *one thing I know*—from the statement of the man who encountered Jesus and relayed to the authorities, "Whether he is a sinner I do not know. One thing I do know, that though I was blind, now I see" (John 9:25). Second, *one thing I do*—from Paul's statement about perseverance: "one thing I do: forgetting what lies behind and straining forward to what lies ahead . . ." (Phil. 3:13). Third, *one thing I ask*—from the psalmist's prayer: "One thing have I asked of the LORD, that will I seek after: that I may dwell in the house of the LORD all the days of my life, to gaze upon the beauty of the LORD and to inquire in his temple" (Ps. 27:4).

The book closes with two interviews I conducted during the con-ference from which this book originated (September 28–29, 2007). The first was with John Piper and John MacArthur, the second with all of the contributors minus MacArthur. The transcripts are lightly edited but still retain the feel of the actual conversations. Our hope is that these sessions will give you a bit of personal insight into these men and women who are seeking to endure and are teaching us to do the same.

Blessings and Benedictions for Our Readers

Have you ever noticed that many of the biblical benedictions and blessings concern God's keeping and your persevering? Toward that end, we pray the following may be true of all those who take up this book:

> The Lord bless you and keep you. . . . (Num. 6:24)

> Now may the God of peace himself sanctify you completely, and may your whole spirit and soul and body be kept blameless at the coming of our Lord Jesus Christ. He who calls you is faithful; he will surely do it. (1 Thess. 5:23–24)

> Now may the God of peace who brought again from the dead our Lord Jesus, the great shepherd of the sheep, by the blood of the eternal covenant, equip you with everything good that you may do his will, working in us that which is pleasing in his sight, through Jesus Christ, to whom be glory forever and ever. Amen. (Heb. 13:20–21)

> Now to him who is able to keep you from stumbling and to present you blameless before the presence of his glory with great joy, to the only God, our Savior, through Jesus Christ our Lord, be glory, majesty, dominion, and authority, before all time and now and forever. Amen. (Jude 24–25)

Amen.

Chapter 1

Four Essentials for Finishing Well

Jerry Bridges

As we think of the endurance of the saints, of enduring to the end and finishing well, there is no better example in Scripture than that of the apostle Paul. As he sat chained in a Roman prison, anticipating an imminent execution, he wrote to Timothy:

> For I am already being poured out as a drink offering, and the time of my departure has come. I have fought the good fight, I have finished the race, I have kept the faith. Henceforth there is laid up for me the crown of righteousness, which the Lord, the righteous judge, will award to me on that Day, and not only to me but also to all who have loved his appearing. (2 Tim. 4:6–8)

Paul was confident he had endured to the end and had finished well. Sadly, however, just a few sentences later he had to write of one of his coworkers: "Demas, in love with this present world, has deserted me and gone to Thessalonica" (2 Tim. 4:10).

Here were two men who had ministered together—Paul and Demas—mentor and mentoree. One endured and finished the race and looked forward to the crown of righteousness. The other man peeled off, deserted his mentor, and was never heard from again. We don't know what finally happened to Demas. We don't know whether he ever repented or not, but the Scripture ends with the fact that "Demas, in love with this present world, has deserted me." In Philemon 24 Paul calls Demas a fellow worker along with Mark and

Aristarchus and Luke. Demas was apparently a promising young man with a promising future; yet as far as we know he did not make it to the end.

This is a sobering thought because many readers of this book are young, committed followers of Jesus Christ. In God's gracious providence you have many years ahead of you, and you expect to finish the race, to stand firm, to endure to the end. But there was a time when Demas also thought that way. He didn't initially join Paul's team with the intention that he would later desert Paul when the going got tough. No, he undoubtedly expected to also stand firm and finish well.

This is a sobering thought even for those of us who are older because, as the famous baseball player Yogi Berra once said, "It ain't over till it's over." So we cannot presume that even at our age we will finish well. We never finish until the day we die. And so all of us, young or old, need to heed the warning that comes to us from the example of Demas.

Four Essential Elements for Finishing Well

Over the last few years I have given a lot of thought to how one finishes well. Although a number of things could be said, I have come to the conclusion that there are four fundamental actions we can take to help us finish well. There may be other issues that are important, but I believe these four are fundamental. They are:

- daily time of focused personal communion with God
- daily appropriation of the gospel
- daily commitment to God as a living sacrifice
- firm belief in the sovereignty and love of God

Now these four essentials are viewed from our perspective; that is, these are things we must and should do or believe. But standing over all of them is the grace of God. The same apostle who said, "I have fought the good fight, I have finished the race, I have kept the faith" also said in another context, "But by the grace of God I am what I am" (1 Cor. 15:10). Paul attributed all of his endurance, all of his faithfulness, to the grace of God. And so as we look at our responsibility, keep in mind that we are enabled to fulfill that responsibility only by the grace of God.

Now the grace of God is often misunderstood. I think one of the most common misunderstandings of the grace of God is, "God's cutting me some slack. Grace is God's letting me get away with a few things." That's the furthest thought from the grace of God. The grace of God comes to us through Jesus Christ as a result of his sinless life and sin-bearing death for us, but that grace is more than just God's kindness and benevolent feeling toward us. The grace of God is dynamic. The grace of God is God in action for our good. And so when the apostle Paul said, "By the grace of God I am what I am," he was speaking about the empowering of the Holy Spirit that God in his grace supplies to each of us as we seek to live for him. So keep in mind as we look at our responsibilities that we can carry out those responsibilities only by the grace of God. In the words of John Newton in his beloved hymn "Amazing Grace," "'Tis grace has brought me safe thus far, and grace will lead me home." At the end of the day when all is said and done, we attribute our faithfulness to the grace of God. So as we consider these four essentials, keep in mind that we practice them only by his grace. Now let's look at them one by one.

A Daily Time of Focused Communion with God

The first essential is a daily time of focused personal communion with God. Many readers are familiar with the old classic *Practicing the Presence of God*, and that is an excellent habit to cultivate. But the foundation of that has to be a time of focused personal communion with God, and it needs to be daily. Demas didn't just wake up one day and make a 90-degree turn. That doesn't happen. Demas drifted little by little toward the attractions of the world. And if you and I do not practice this daily focused time of communion with God, we will find ourselves also drifting in the wrong direction.

In my Navy days before we had global positioning satellites we used a sexton to get our navigational position twice each day. At dawn and at dusk we would "shoot the stars" and get a position. And invariably after having done that, we had to make a minor course correction. Obviously if we didn't do that, not only daily but in our case twice a day, we would soon find that we were way off course.

You and I also need that daily course correction, and we do this as we have this focused time with God. Demas was in love with this present world. Each of us, whether believer or unbeliever, is in love with something. Demas was in love with the world. The apostle John said, "Do not love the world" (1 John 2:15). But we cannot just "not love the world" and have a vacuum in our hearts. In order to not love the world we have to love God. And our time of daily focused communion with God is a time when that love of God and his love for us is refreshed in our hearts.

Consider the words of the psalmist. In Psalm 63:1 he says, "O God, you are my God; earnestly I seek you; my soul thirsts for you; my flesh faints for you, as in a dry and weary land where there is no water." Notice the intensity of those words, *Earnestly I seek you; my soul thirsts for you; my flesh faints for you.* This is far more than just a daily Bible reading and going over a few prayer requests, our "quiet time" or our "morning devotions" or something like that. While I'm not negating those terms, keep in mind the fact that the purpose of that quiet time is not just to read a chapter in the Bible and go over a few prayer requests. Rather it should be a time of personal communion with God. Obviously we need a plan. We don't just open our Bible and point our finger at a passage of Scripture and say, this is my passage for today. But communion with God is far, far more than a plan. Communion with God is meeting with him. It is asking God to speak to us. It is speaking to him as we read his Word, as we interact with his Word in prayer, as we pray over what God is saying to us in his Word.

Psalm 42:1–2 says something similar: "As a deer pants for flowing streams, so pants my soul for you, O God. My soul thirsts for God, for the living God. When shall I come and appear before God?"

Or again David in Psalm 27:4 said: "One thing have I asked of the LORD, that will I seek after: that I may dwell in the house of the LORD all the days of my life, to gaze upon the beauty of the LORD and to inquire in his temple." The beauty of the Lord is not a physical beauty. It's the beauty of his attributes. It's the beauty of the cross. It's the beauty of what he has done for us in Christ. And the psalmist said, I just want to gaze upon the beauty of the Lord; I want to have communion with God. This is what the focused time is all about. All of these Scriptures speak of an intense desire to have that personal communion with God.

Now it's helpful to have a plan, but the plan must direct you to God himself. Do we spend time with God or do we just read a chapter in the Bible? Spending time with God certainly involves the reading of a chapter or three verses or three chapters or whatever. But the object of that is to meet with God, to have God speak to us and to respond to him. As I open my Bible each day, I ask, "Lord, may I today spend time with you. Would you speak to me from your Word? Would you encourage me? Would you teach me? Would you rebuke me if I need it? Lord, whatever you see that I need today, I come to spend time with you." Then as I begin to read the passage I respond to God over what I'm reading. I pray back to him whatever is appropriate in that passage.

If you read through the Psalms, you will notice that in most of them the psalmist is either speaking to God or speaking about God. But usually he is speaking to God. Sometimes he's rejoicing, and sometimes he's lamenting. He says, for example, "O God, why do you hide your face from me?" (cf. Ps. 88:4). He is interacting with God. This is what we want to do. And as we daily seek to have that personal communion with God, God will give us that navigational fix, so to speak, and he will show us what course corrections we need to make in our lives so that we do not drift off course. And so if you and I are going to endure to the end, we must make it a practice—a discipline, if you please—to have that focused, daily communion with God.

In 1988 my first wife was dying of cancer after a long illness. One morning as I was struggling with the reality of her approaching death, there came to my mind, "Psalm 116:15, 'Precious in the sight of the LORD is the death of his saints.'" With that came the realization that God himself had an interest in what was happening to my wife. For me I would be losing my sweetheart, but for God, it would be the homecoming of one of his children.

I thought of the time when our fifteen-year-old son went on an eleven-week summer missions program and how we eagerly antici-pated his coming home. I realized that as incredible as it seems, God eagerly awaits the homecoming of his children. And then there came to mind a part of Psalm 16:11, "in your presence there is fullness of joy; at your right hand are pleasures forevermore." As I prayed over that Scripture, I realized that very soon Eleanor would experience the incredible joy of actually being in the very presence of God.

As I continued to pray back to God, I said something like, "Father, you will gain one of your children coming home, and Eleanor will gain being in your presence forevermore, but what about me?" Quickly there came to mind words from 1 Thessalonians 4:13 in the King James Version, "ye sorrow not, even as others which have no hope."

With that assurance from God and his Word, I was able to emotionally release her. Two weeks later she died. In the aftermath of her death I sorrowed, but not as one who has no hope. Meanwhile I was comforted by the assurance that God had joyously welcomed one of his children home and that she was enjoying his presence forevermore.

I never experienced the various stages of grief that so many people go through after the death of a loved one. I never became angry at God or experienced days of depression. Within a week or so I was able to resume my normal responsibilities in my work. All of this because years before I had established the practice of a daily time of personal communion with God.

I should warn against the possibility of becoming legalistic about our time of communion with God. That is, we do not earn blessings from God because we have this time, nor do we forfeit his blessing on a day we miss it. God does not bless *because* we spend time with him, but he often blesses *through* that time, as he did when my wife was approaching death.

Nor should we expect to always have God speak to us through his Word in such a dramatic fashion as I experienced that day. As with the navigational course corrections aboard ship, God's spiritual course corrections in our lives are usually incremental and not especially dramatic. But they are necessary.

A Daily Appropriation of the Gospel

The second essential is a daily appropriation of the gospel. I have put personal communion with God first to highlight its priority because that's the absolute basic essential. But in actual practice I put my daily appropriation of the gospel first. That is, I begin my time with

God by reviewing and appropriating to myself the gospel. Since the gospel is only for sinners, I come to Christ as a still practicing sinner. In fact, I usually use the words of that tax collector in the temple when he cried out, "God, be merciful to me, a sinner" (Luke 18:13). God has been merciful, and I'm quick to acknowledge his mercy in my life, but I say to him that I come in the attitude of that tax collector. "I need your mercy. I am still a practicing sinner. Even my very best deeds are sinful in your sight, and I am an object of your mercy and your grace."

It's important that we come, first of all, by appropriating the gospel because it's through Christ that we have access to God the Father. Paul says in Ephesians 2:18, "For through him we both [Jew and Gentile] have access in one Spirit to the Father." We cannot come directly to God. We must always come through the blood of the Lord Jesus Christ. But God not only *allows* us to come; he *invites* us to come. The writer of Hebrews says, "Therefore, brothers, since we have confidence to enter the holy places by the blood of Jesus, by the new and living way that he opened for us through the curtain, that is, through his flesh, and since we have a great priest over the house of God, let us draw near with a true heart in full assurance of faith" (Heb. 10:19–22). And so as we appropriate the gospel it gives us the confidence to come into the very presence of God to have communion with him. So we need to learn to live by the gospel every day of our lives.

In the early years of my Christian life and even in my early ministry I regarded the gospel as a message for the unbeliever. Now that I was a Christian I personally no longer needed the gospel except as a message to share with unbelievers. But I learned the hard way many years ago that I need the gospel every day of my life.

At the time I was serving overseas, and I was single and lonely. Additionally I was struggling with some interpersonal relationship issues. Every Monday night I led a Bible study at an American Air Force base about an hour's drive from where I lived. And every Monday night as I drove home, Satan would attack me with accusations of my sin. Out of desperation I began to resort to the gospel. To use an expression I learned years later, I began to "preach the gospel to myself." And I subsequently learned that I continued to need the gospel every day of my life. That is why I list this practice as one of the four essential elements.

Consider Paul's words in Galatians 2:20. The apostle writes, "I have been crucified with Christ. It is no longer I who live, but Christ who lives in me. And the life I now live in the flesh I live by faith in the Son of God, who loved me and gave himself for me." The context of this verse is the subject of justification. In verses 15–17 Paul speaks of our being justified four times. He says we're not justified by works of the law but by faith in Jesus Christ, and he keeps repeating that thought. And then in verse 21 he says, "I do not nullify the grace of God, for if justification were through the law, then Christ died for no purpose." Clearly in this entire passage, verses 15–21, he is talking about the subject of justification. He is going to get to sanctification later, but that's not in this context. The reason I make a point of that is because I want to call your attention particularly to the last sentence of verse 20. "And the life I now live in the flesh I live by faith in the Son of God, who loved me and gave himself for me." Remember, in the context Paul is speaking about justification, not sanctification.

Now this raises an apparent problem or question. That is, we know that justification is a point-in-time past event. At the time you trusted Christ you were at that precise moment declared righteous by God. You were justified. That's why Paul in Romans 5:1 can speak of justification in the past tense when he says, "Therefore, since we have been justified by faith, we have peace with God through our Lord Jesus Christ." And yet here in this passage he speaks of it in the present tense. "The life that I *now* live in the flesh," today. The life that I live today, "I live by faith in the Son of God, who loved me and gave himself for me." So if justification is a point-in-time event that happened in our past, why does Paul speak of it in the present tense? The life that I *now* live today I live by faith in the Son of God.

The answer to that question is one of the most important truths we can learn about the gospel. For the apostle Paul, justification was not only a *past event*; it was also a *present reality*. This is where so many Christians miss it. They can look back to the day that they trusted Christ. And if you press them on that they will say, "Yes, I was justified at that time." But today they seek to live their lives as if it depends upon them. In their mind they have reverted to a performance relationship with God. And so the thinking is, if I had my quiet time and if I haven't had any lustful thoughts and these kind of things, then I expect God to bless me today. We want to pay our own way. We want to earn God's blessings. The apostle Paul didn't do that. Paul looked outside himself and saw himself clothed in the righteousness of Christ. He saw himself declared righteous. We say to a person who trusts Christ, "You have been justified. You've been declared righteous. Your sins have been forgiven. You stand before God today clothed in the righteousness of Jesus Christ." And then we can point to eternity and say, "When you go to be with the Lord forever, you will still stand clothed in the righteousness of Jesus Christ." Even though we will have left our sinful nature behind, even though we will be righteous people made perfect, as the writer of Hebrews says (Heb. 12:23), we will for all eternity stand in the righteousness of Christ. That never changes.

But what about from the time of our conversion until the time we go to be with the Lord? For most Christians it's a performance relationship. That is why we need a daily appropriation of the gospel, because it is our nature to drift toward a performance relationship. Going back to those days of crossing the Pacific Ocean and getting those navigational positions twice a day, if we did not get those we would drift slowly off course. And if you do not daily appropriate the gospel, you will drift toward a performance relationship with God. And when you do that, you lead yourself in one of two directions. If you have a very superficial view of sin in your life—that is, if you think of sin in terms of the big gross sins that society outside of us commits—then you will tend toward religious pride because you're not doing those things. But if you are conscientious and if you're seeing some of these "respectable" sins, such as gossip and pride, jealousy and envy and a critical spirit and these kind of things, if you're seeing those in your life and you do not live by the gospel, that can lead you to despair. And so oftentimes people in this second category just kind of slack off because they can't handle the tension. They can't handle the difference between what they know they should be and what they honestly see themselves to be. And what resolves that tension is the gospel, which reminds us that our sins are forgiven and that we are clothed in the righteousness of Jesus Christ. At the same time, that which keeps us from spiritual pride is the gospel, because again the gospel is only for sinners. But we are all sinners, still practicing sinners, even though we've been delivered from the guilt and the dominion of sin. Yes, that's true. And we are now called *saints*, separated ones. But we still sin in thought, word, deed, and most of all in motive because we often do the right thing for a wrong reason or for a mixed reason. We want to please God, but we want to look good in the process. And so we come to the Lord and we say, "Lord, I come still a practicing sinner, but I look to Jesus Christ and his shed blood and his perfect obedience, his righteous life that has been credited to me. And I see myself standing before you clothed in his righteousness."

That will get you out of bed in the morning. That will get you excited about the Christian life, when you see yourself daily clothed in his righteousness. And that will keep you from loving the world. You can't love the gospel and love the world at the same time. So a daily appropriation of the gospel will keep you from getting off course.

About a hundred years ago a great theologian by the name of B. B. Warfield, who was a professor at Princeton Theological Seminary, wrote these words: "There is nothing in us or done by us at any stage of our earthly development because of which we are acceptable to God." Warfield is saying there is nothing that we do in ourselves that makes us acceptable to God. He continues: "We must always be accepted for Christ's sake, or we cannot ever be accepted at all." Then he continues, and this is important: "This is not true of us only when we believe. It is just as true after we have believed. It will continue to be true as long as we live. Our need of Christ does not cease with our believing; nor does the nature of our relation to Him or to God through Him ever alter, no matter what our attainments in Christian graces or our achievement in Christian behavior may be."[1] What he is saying is that it doesn't matter how sanctified we become. It doesn't matter how much we grow in the Christian life. He says it is always on Christ's blood and righteousness alone that we can rest.

One of the sins I struggle with frequently is the sin of anxiety; not anxiety in general, but anxiety over delayed luggage on airplane

---

[1]B. B. Warfield, *The Works of Benjamin B. Warfield*, 10 vols. (Grand Rapids, MI: Baker, 1931; reprint 1991), 7:113.

trips. I have had so many bad experiences with my luggage not arriving with me on the same flight that I no longer assume my bag will arrive with me. Every time I go to the baggage claim area I have to pray against the sin of anxiety.

A few years ago, after two back-to-back really bad experiences, I said to my wife, "I have to confess I'm just an anxious person." The next morning in my time with God I was reading in Matthew 8. Part of that chapter is the account of Jesus and the disciples caught in a great storm on the Sea of Galilee. In verse 24 the text says that a great storm arose, "so that the boat was being swamped by the waves; but *he [that is, Jesus] was asleep.*" I was arrested by the statement that Jesus was asleep in the midst of this raging storm while the disciples were terrified.

As I pondered that scene the thought came to me, *Jesus was asleep in the boat for me.* By that I mean that all that Jesus did in both his sinless life and sin-bearing death, he did as our representative and substitute. His perfect obedience as well as his death was all on our behalf. In contrast to my sin of anxiety over missing luggage, Jesus was never anxious. In far more desperate circumstances than mine, he fully trusted his Heavenly Father. And I get the credit for it. By his death he paid for the sin and guilt of my anxiety. And by his perfect trust he clothed me with his righteousness.

So I left my time with God that morning not feeling guilty because of my persistent struggle with anxiety but feeling encouraged because I knew my sin was forgiven and instead I had been credited with perfect obedience (in this case, the perfect trust) of Jesus. So I went out into my day not only encouraged but determined that by his grace I would fight against my anxiety.

That's what it means to live by the gospel. That's why we need to appropriate the gospel every day of our lives, because God only accepts us for Christ's sake. God sees us clothed in the righteousness of Christ, and he wants us to see ourselves clothed in the righteousness of Christ, so that we will come to him on that basis and seek to relate to him through the merit of the Lord Jesus Christ and not through our own works. All of us in our sinful nature are prone to slide toward a works-based relationship with God. And even though I have been preaching this kind of message for many years, I can tell you honestly it is so easy to revert in that direction because of our sinful human nature. It is our sinful nature that thinks we must somehow earn God's favor by our own hard work or our own faithfulness. Now we want to be faithful, we want to work hard, but not in order to earn God's approval, but because we have God's approval. And so a daily appropriation of the gospel is essential to enduring to the end.

A Daily Commitment to God as a Living Sacrifice

The third essential is a daily commitment to God as a living sacrifice. And for that I direct your attention to Romans 12:1: "I appeal to you therefore, brothers, by the mercies of God, to present your bodies as a living sacrifice, holy and acceptable to God, which is your spiritual worship." As we daily reflect on the gospel and what God has done for us in Christ, this should lead us to present ourselves as daily, living sacrifices.

In using the word *sacrifice* Paul was obviously drawing from the Old Testament sacrificial system. Those sacrifices are set forth for us in the book of Leviticus, and all of them together portrayed the one great sacrifice of the Lord Jesus Christ. Whether or not Paul had in mind a particular sacrifice, one of them, I think, best helps us understand what Paul is saying when he says to present our bodies as living sacrifices. That is the burnt offering. I think the burnt offering helps us understand what Paul is saying because two things were unique about the burnt offering. First, of all of the animal offerings, the burnt offering was the only one in which the entire animal was consumed upon the altar. With the others, only certain portions were burned on the altar, and the remaining portions were reserved for the priests or even in one case for the offerer and his family. But with the burnt offering the entire animal was consumed upon the altar. And for that reason it was called the whole burnt offering. And it signified not only atonement for sin but also consecration or dedication of the offerer to God. Also, the priests on duty were to present a burnt offering twice a day, in the morning and in the evening, so that the fire would not go out upon the altar (cf. Lev. 6:8–13). In other words, there was always a burnt offering being consumed upon the altar. And so for that reason it has been called a continual burnt offering. So there were two descriptive terms—a whole burnt offering and a continual burnt offering. And I think that you can readily see the application that can be drawn from that.

First of all, the whole burnt offering would signify that we are to consecrate *our entire being*, not only ourselves but all that we have. Everything about us we are to consecrate, to dedicate to God, to present to him as a sacrifice. Then the word *continually* (Lev. 6:13; Heb. 10:1) says to us that this must be repeated constantly. Just as we have a tendency to revert to a works-based relationship with God, we have a tendency to want to take back that which we have committed to God. Often in a moment of high spiritual emotion we might sincerely and honestly say, "Lord, I give my whole being, my body, my mind, my service, my money, everything about me, Lord, I consecrate it all to you." And then we go out and in a few weeks we're confronted with some issue, and we tend to draw back, and we realize that we're not as consecrated as we thought we were. Daily renewal of this consecration helps us to keep from doing that.

The second word that's significant in Romans 12:1 is the word *present*. Paul says to "*present* your bodies as a living sacrifice." Some translations use a different word, but whatever word is used, the idea is to give over to or to put at another's disposal.

Some years ago when our son and daughter-in-law were expecting their first child they had as their sole means of transportation a pickup truck. My wife and I realized they could not put an infant seat in that pickup. And though he is an engineer, our son was teaching part-time as a lecturer at the local university in order to have more time for ministry among the large Muslim population in the area. We knew they could not afford to buy another car, so we decided to give them one of our two cars. We drove that car to their city and took the title with us. When we got there, we signed the title over to our son and daughter-in-law. At that time the car legally became theirs. We presented it to them.

But not only did we legally transfer the title, we transferred it emotionally as well. That is, once we signed the title over to them, in our minds it was their car to do with as they pleased. We knew that in another year or so they would be leaving the USA to minister overseas. We knew that at that time they would sell the car and use the proceeds as part of their passage money. And it never occurred to us to think, *When they sell that car we'll get the money because, after all, it was our car.* When we signed that title we not only made a legal transaction, we made an emotional transaction.

Now fast-forward a few years, and they were coming home on furlough for three months. Again Jane and I realized they were going to need a car while they were here. We had replaced the car that we had previously given them, so again we had two cars. And we decided that we would loan them one of our cars. It happened to be my car that was loaned. During those three months I had mixed emotions. On the one hand, I was happy that we could provide them with the car they needed. On the other hand, I missed my car since I had to always arrange with Jane to use hers.

Now God has not asked us to loan ourselves temporarily to him. He's asked us to present ourselves to him as living sacrifices to use as he pleases. The fact is, objectively this has already taken place. The apostle Paul tells us in 1 Corinthians 6:19–20, "You are not your own, for you were bought with a price." Paul wants us to affirm in our hearts and in our emotions what is true in reality, but he approaches it by way of an appeal. He does not say, "This is your duty to do." He does not say, "You're not your own; you don't have a choice in the matter." He says, "I appeal to you . . . by the mercies of God."

We see something similar in the short letter of Paul to Philemon. To review the story, Philemon owned a slave named Onesimus. At some point prior to this letter, Onesimus had deserted Philemon and had probably stolen from him in the process. He had made his way from what is now modern-day Turkey across Greece all the way to Italy, and there he encountered Paul in Rome during Paul's first imprisonment. There Paul led him to Christ and discipled him. But Paul realized there was an issue. Onesimus needed to make things right with Philemon. So Paul sent Onesimus back to Philemon, but he sent with him this letter. The purpose of the letter was to ask Philemon to receive Onesimus, to forgive him for having run away and probably having stolen as well, and not only to forgive him but now to receive him as a brother. Now that's quite a thing to ask, so this is the way Paul approaches it: "Accordingly, though I am bold enough in Christ to command you to do what is required, yet for love's sake I prefer to appeal to you" (Philem. 8–9). Paul could have said, "Philemon, you don't really have a choice. It is your Christian duty to forgive and receive Onesimus." But Paul didn't approach Philemon that way. Instead he appealed "for love's sake." He wanted Philemon to desire to do what it was his duty to do. He did not want to coerce Philemon. And so he appealed to Philemon to do for love's sake that which he should do in obedience to the command of God.

In the same way, the apostle Paul appeals to us. He says, "I appeal to you . . . by the mercies of God." Do you want to know what the mercy of God looks like? Read the first five verses of Ephesians 2. We were dead in trespasses and sins. We were absolutely helpless. We were not just sick—we were dead. We were slaves to the world and to Satan and to the passions of our flesh. And we were by nature objects of God's wrath. That was our condition. That's why we needed mercy. And then Paul says, "But God, being rich in mercy, because of the great love with which he loved us . . . made us alive together with Christ." That's mercy.

Do you see yourself today as an object of God's mercy? Do you realize that apart from his mercy you would be headed for eternal damnation? That's why Paul says, "I appeal to you . . . by the mercies of God."

Presenting our bodies as living sacrifices is not something that we check off and say, "Well, I've done that; it's my duty to do." It should be a spontaneous response to our appropriation of the gospel. We are talking about communion with God. We are talking about being embraced by his love and his mercy and his grace. And we see that in the gospel. The apostle John said that God showed his love to us by sending his Son to be the propitiation for our sins (1 John 4:10)—that is, to exhaust the wrath of God that you and I should have experienced. As we daily appropriate the gospel, we bask in his love, and genuinely basking in his love will lead us to present our bodies as living sacrifices. But that has to be renewed daily. We can't live today on yesterday's commitment.

The outworking of presenting our bodies as living sacrifices will be different for each of us. For some it might mean reducing one's standard of living in order to be able to give more to God's kingdom work. For our son, it meant taking a lower-paying job in order to have more time for ministry. For me at this time, it means being willing to continually give myself to the ministry God has given me.

At the time of this writing, it is only a couple of weeks until my seventy-eighth birthday. Over the past dozen years I have flown over a million miles, I have delivered over a thousand messages, I have written several books and a number of articles for Christian magazines. I confess I often get weary of the continuous travel, the frequent writing deadlines, and the pressure of constant message preparations, and I sometimes begin to feel sorry for myself.

How do I keep going? How do I keep from feeling sorry for myself? Each day as I appropriate the gospel for myself, I say to God, "I am your servant. Because of your mercy to me and your grace at work in me, I again present my body as a living sacrifice. If this means continual travel and continual time pressure, I accept that from you and thank you for the privilege of being in your ministry."

In fact my life verse is Ephesians 3:8, "To me, though I am the very least of all the saints, this grace was given, to preach to the Gentiles the unsearchable riches of Christ." I am not only a recipient of the grace of the gospel; I also have the privilege of teaching it to others. So through my appropriation of the gospel to myself, my "living sacrifice" becomes a privilege. I am constantly in awe that God would give me the privilege of teaching many Christians that the gospel is not just for unbelievers but for them to live by every day.

A Firm Belief in the Sovereignty and Love of God

The fourth essential is a firm belief in the sovereignty and love of God. This essential doesn't have the word *daily* in it, but it must be practiced continually. Years ago M. Scott Peck wrote a book (*The Road Less Traveled*) that began with a three-word sentence: "Life is difficult." Most people would agree with that. If you've lived very long you realize life is difficult, or at least it's often difficult, and sometimes it's even painful. And over time you will experience both difficulties and pain. So if you want to endure to the end, if you want to stand firm in the face of life's difficulties and pain, then you must have a firm belief in the sovereignty and the love of God. You must not only believe that God is in control of every event in his universe and specifically every event in your own life, but that God, in exercising that control, does so from his infinite love for you.

Many passages show us the sovereignty and love of God, but I have chosen Lamentations 3:37–38. "Who has spoken and it came to pass, unless the Lord has commanded it? Is it not from the mouth of the Most High that good and bad come?" I've chosen this particular passage because verse 37 ("Who has spoken and it came to pass, unless the Lord has commanded it?") affirms God's sovereignty over the actions of other people. So much of life's pain is caused by the sinful actions of other people. And if you do not believe that God is sovereign and in control of those actions, you will be tempted to become bitter. And if you become bitter, you begin to turn aside from God, and you will not stand firm. You will not endure if you let other people's sinful actions cause you to become bitter. And one of the ways we can keep from becoming bitter is to realize that God is in sovereign control even over the sinful actions of other people.

Joseph is the classic illustration of this. Three times in Genesis 45 (especially vv. 5–8), after Joseph had revealed himself to his brothers he told them that God had been in control all the way along. For example, "It was not you who sent me here, but God" (v. 8). And then in Genesis 50:20 he says, "You meant evil against me, but God meant it for good." Joseph believed in the sovereignty of God, even in the sinful actions of his brothers.

At one time I suffered a crushing and humiliating disappointment in my work situation. It certainly was not due to the sinful actions of other people, but it was due to their thoughtless and uncaring actions. This action occurred on a Thursday afternoon, and I was scheduled to speak at a weekend conference beginning Friday night. How could I possibly recover from the hurt and humiliation so as to be able to speak Friday evening?

On Friday morning I awakened with the words of Job in my mind, "The Lord gave, and the Lord has taken away" (Job 1:21). In my time with God that morning I was able to say, "Lord, in times past you gave, but now you have taken it all away. I accept this as from you." My turbulent emotions quieted down, and I was able to speak at the conference as if nothing had happened. And I never became at all bitter toward those other people. This was because I believed in the sovereign control of God in their actions.

Secondly, Lamentations 3:38 says to us, "Is it not from the mouth of the Most High that good and bad come?" That is, God is in sovereign control over the difficulties and the pain just as much as he is in control over what we would consider to be the good things, the blessings of this life. Now we should thank God for the good things of life. We are to be thankful people. But what about the bad things, the things that we would not choose to have in our lives? Paul tells us in 1 Thessalonians 5:18 to "give thanks in all circumstances," and then he adds, "for this is the will of God in Christ Jesus for you." That is to say, it is the moral will of God that we give thanks in all circumstances. In 4:3 he said, "This is the will of God . . . that you abstain from sexual immorality." Obviously that's speaking of the moral will of God. And Paul uses this same phraseology in 5:18 where he says, "For this is the will of God in Christ Jesus for you." It is the moral will of God that we give thanks in all circumstances.

How do we do this? We do it by faith. We don't just grit our teeth and say, "Lord, I don't feel thankful, but you said to give thanks, so I'm going to give you thanks even though I don't feel thankful." That's not giving thanks. We do it by faith. We do it by trusting in the promises of God. We do it by faith in the words of God through Paul in Romans 8:28–29, where he says "God causes all things to work together for good to those who love him." And then he defines the good in verse 29 as being conformed to the likeness of the Lord Jesus Christ. This is what God is after. He wants to conform us to the likeness of Christ; so he brings or allows these various circumstances, circumstances that we ourselves would not choose. He brings them into our lives because he wants to use those circumstances in his way to conform us more and more to the likeness of Christ. And so by faith we can say, "Lord, I do not know what particular purpose you have in this difficulty or this pain, this trial. But you said that you will use it to conform me more and more to Jesus Christ, and for that I give you thanks." So we give thanks by faith.

We also do it by faith in the promise that he will never leave us or forsake us. The writer of Hebrews quotes from the Old Testament when he says, "For he has said, 'I will never leave you nor forsake you'" (13:5). That word *never* is an absolute word. It doesn't mean sometimes or most of the time; it means never. You can count on that. God, who cannot lie, has said, "I will never leave you or forsake you. I may allow or put you in this very difficult and painful situation, but I will not forsake you." Then we can look ahead to Romans 8:38–39, a passage that we can summarize as saying that God has said that nothing in all creation will be able to separate us from his love in Christ Jesus.

It's possible that sometime in your life things will totally fall apart and you will feel that you have nothing left. Let me tell you, there are two things that God will never take away. *God will never take away the gospel.* In the most difficult days of your life you still stand before God clothed in the righteousness of Christ. Your sins are forgiven. Even your doubts are forgiven because Christ fully trusted the Father on your behalf. And, second, *God will never take away his promises.* These two assurances will remain even if everything else is stripped away. If you were brought to the point of being like Job, this you can count on. You stand before God clothed in the righteousness of Christ. He will never, never take the gospel away from you. And you will always have his promise, "never will I leave you; never will I forsake you."

Conclusion: Persevering, Not Just Enduring, to the End

These are the four essentials. I'm sure there are other important considerations, but I believe these are fundamental. And so I would commend them to you:

- a daily time of focused communion with God,
- a daily appropriation of the gospel,
- a daily presenting yourself as a living sacrifice, and
- a continual firm belief in the sovereignty and the goodness of God.

Then finally I want to inject another word for our consideration in the subject of standing firm or enduring to the end. That's the word *perseverance*. The word *perseverance* is very similar in meaning to the word *endurance*, and often we equate the two. But there can be a subtle difference. The word *endure* means to stand firm, and that is the theme of this book. We are to stand firm. We're not to be carried about with every wind of doctrine theologically. We're not to go off to this and that and the other. We're to stand firm. But we need to do more than stand. We need to move forward. When Paul says, "I have finished the race" (2 Tim. 4:7), obviously he was talking about motion. And perseverance means to keep going in spite of obstacles. So when Paul says, "I have finished the race," basically he was saying, "I have persevered." We do need to stand firm, and Scripture over and over again exhorts us to stand firm. But remember, that's more than just standing still. If we get that idea, we've missed the point. We must move forward. We must persevere. We must be like Paul and say, "I have fought the good fight, I have finished the race, I have kept the faith." May you and I be like the apostle Paul.

> Our Father, again we come back to the realization that any of us could become a Demas, and it's only by your grace that any of us stands firm. And so, Father, we acknowledge our total dependence upon you. We acknowledge our total indebtedness to you. And we give you thanks for your grace. But also, Father, we acknowledge our responsibility, and we pray that by your grace we will fulfill our responsibility, that we will practice these disciplines that will enable us to stand firm and to finish the race. In Jesus' name, Amen.

Chapter 2

Getting Old to the Glory of God

John Piper

So even to old age and gray hairs,
O God, do not forsake me,
until I proclaim your might to another generation,
your power to all those to come.

PSALM 71:18

Getting old to the glory of God means getting old in a way that makes God look glorious. It means living and dying in a way that shows God to be the all-satisfying Treasure that he is. So it would include, for example, not living in ways that make this world look like your treasure. Which means that most of the suggestions that this world offers us for our retirement years are bad ideas. They call us to live in a way that would make this world look like our treasure. And when that happens, God is belittled.

Resolutely Resisting Retirement

Getting old to the glory of God means resolutely resisting the typical American dream of retirement. It means being so satisfied with all that God promises to be for us in Christ that we are set free from the cravings that create so much emptiness and uselessness in retirement. Instead, knowing that we have an infinitely satisfying and everlasting inheritance in God just over the horizon of life makes us zealous in our few remaining years here to spend ourselves in the sacrifices of love, not the accumulation of comforts.

The Perseverance of Raymond Lull

Consider the way Raymond Lull finished his earthly course.

Raymond Lull was born into a wealthy family on the island of Majorca off the coast of Spain in 1235. His life as a youth was dissolute, but a series of visions compelled him to follow Christ. He first entered monastic life but later became a missionary to Muslim countries in northern Africa. He learned Arabic and after returning from Africa became a professor of Arabic until he was seventy-nine. Samuel Zwemer describes the end of his life like this, and, of course, it is the exact opposite of retirement:

> His pupils and friends naturally desired that he should end his days in the peaceful pursuit of learning and the comfort of companionship.
>
> Such however was not Lull's wish. . . . In Lull's contemplations we read . . . "Men are wont to die, O Lord, from old age, the failure of natural warmth and excess of cold; but thus, if it be Thy will, Thy servant would not wish to die; he would prefer to die in the glow of love, even as Thou wast willing to die for him."
>
> The dangers and difficulties that made Lull shrink back . . . in 1291 only urged him forward to North Africa once more in 1314. His love had not grown cold, but burned the brighter. . . . He longed not only for the martyr's crown, but also once more to see his little band of believers [in Africa]. Animated by these sentiments he crossed over to Bugia [Algeria] on August 14, and for nearly a whole year labored secretly among a little circle of converts, whom on his previous visits he had won over to the Christian faith. . . .
>
> At length, weary of seclusion, and longing for martyrdom, he came forth into the open market and presented himself to the people as the same man whom they had once expelled from their town. It was Elijah showing himself to a mob of Ahabs! Lull stood before them and threatened them with divine wrath if they still persisted in their errors. He pleaded with love, but spoke plainly the whole truth. The consequences can be easily anticipated. Filled with fanatic fury at his boldness, and unable to reply to his arguments, the populace seized him, and dragged him out of the town; there by the command, or at least the connivance, of the king, he was stoned on the 30th of June 1315.[1]

---

[1] Samuel Zwemer, *Raymond Lull: First Missionary to the Moslems* (New York: Fleming H. Revell, 1902), 132–145.

So, Raymond Lull was eighty years old when he gave his life for the Muslims of North Africa. Nothing could be further from the American dream of retirement than the way Lull lived out his last days.

Dying to Make Christ Look Great

In John 21:19, Jesus told Peter "by what kind of death he was to glorify God." There are different ways of dying. And there are different ways of living just before we die. But for the Christian, all of them—the final living and the dying—are supposed to make God look glorious. All of them are supposed to show that Christ—not this world—is our supreme Treasure.

So growing old to the glory of God means using whatever strength and eyesight and hearing and mobility and resources we have left to treasure Christ and in that joy to serve people—that is, to seek to bring them with us into the everlasting enjoyment of Christ. Serving people, and not ourselves, as the overflow of treasuring Christ makes Christ look great.

The Fear of Not Persevering

One of the great obstacles to getting old to the glory of God is the fear that we will not persevere in treasuring Christ and loving people—we just won't make it. We won't be able to say with Paul in 2 Timothy 4:7–8, "I have fought the good fight, I have finished the race, I have kept the faith. Henceforth there is laid up for me the crown of righteousness, which the Lord, the righteous judge, will award to me on that Day, and not only to me but also to all who have loved his appearing." The reward of final righteousness will come to those who have loved his appearing, that is, who treasure him supremely and want him to be here. So this treasuring of Christ must be included in and part of the fought-fight and the finished-race and the kept-faith. Faith includes treasuring Christ and his appearing. You don't have faith if you don't want Jesus.

So one great obstacle to getting old to the glory of God is the fear that we can't maintain this treasuring of Christ. And so we fear that we can't bear the fruit of love that flows from faith (Gal. 5:6; 1 Tim.

1:5). We fear that we're not going to make it. And the main reason that this fear of not persevering in faith and love is an obstacle to getting old to the glory of God is that the two most common ways of overcoming this fear are deadly.

Two Deadly Ways to Overcome This Fear

There are two opposite ways to ruin your life in trying to overcome this fear. One is to assume that perseverance in faith and love is not necessary for final salvation. And the other is to assume that perseverance is necessary and then depend on our efforts in some measure to fulfill that necessity and to secure God's favor. Let me show why both of these are devastatingly misguided and deadly, and then what is the biblical way of growing old to the glory of God.

Deadly: "Perseverance Is Unnecessary"

It's a mistake to think that perseverance in faith and love is not necessary for final salvation. A deadly mistake. Jesus said in Mark 13:13, "You will be hated by all for my name's sake. But *the one who endures to the end will be saved.*" Hebrews 12:14 says, "Strive for peace with everyone, and for *the holiness without which no one will see the Lord.*" In Galatians 6:8–9, Paul says, "The one who sows to his own flesh will from the flesh reap corruption, but the one who sows to the Spirit will from the Spirit reap eternal life." So notice that the two reapings are of corruption on the one hand and eternal life on the other hand. Then he says in the next verse, "And let us not grow weary of doing good, for in due season we will reap [eternal life], if we do not give up."

So clearly persevering in the furrows of faith by sowing to the Spirit and bearing his fruit of love is necessary for final salvation. "God chose you," Paul says in 2 Thessalonians 2:13, ". . . to be saved, *through sanctification* by the Spirit and belief in the truth." "*Saved through sanctification*" means that sanctification—the path of love— is the path on which saved sinners go to heaven. And it's the only path that leads to heaven.

So it is a tragic and deadly mistake to try to overcome the fear of not persevering in old age by saying you don't have to persevere.

Deadly: "Perseverance Puts or Keeps God on Our Side"

But the other misguided way of overcoming the fear of not persevering is just as dangerous. It is the way that says: "Yes, perseverance in faith and love is necessary, and that means I must wait till the last day for God to be 100% for me, and I must depend on my efforts to secure God's full favor. God may get me started in the Christian life by faith in him alone, but perseverance happens another way. God makes his ongoing favor depend on my efforts." That, I say, is deadly and leads either to despair or pride. And certainly not to perseverance.

What's wrong with that? You can see what's wrong if you ask this question: When does God become totally and irrevocably for us—not 99%, but 100% for us? Is it at the end of the age, at the Last Day, when he has seen our whole life and measured it to see if it is worthy of his being for us? That is not what the Bible teaches.

What the Bible teaches is that God becomes 100% irrevocably for us at the moment of justification, that is, the moment when we see Christ as a beautiful Savior and receive him as our substitute punishment and our substitute perfection. All of God's wrath, all of the condemnation we deserve, was poured out on Jesus. All of God's demands for perfect righteousness were fulfilled by Christ. The moment we see (by grace!) this Treasure and receive him in this way, his death counts as our death and his condemnation as our condemnation and his righteousness as our righteousness, and God becomes 100% irrevocably for us forever in that instant.

"We hold that one is justified by faith apart from works of the law" (Rom. 3:28). "Therefore, since we have been justified by faith, we have peace with God through our Lord Jesus Christ" (Rom. 5:1). "There is therefore now no condemnation for those who are in Christ Jesus" (Rom. 8:1). So in Christ Jesus—in union with him by faith alone, by receiving all that he is for us—God is totally, 100% irrevocably for us. And the implications of that are spelled out in Romans 8:31–35:

> If God is for us, who can be against us? He who did not spare his own Son but gave him up for us all, how will he not also with him graciously give us all things? Who shall bring any charge against God's elect? It is God who justifies. Who is to condemn? Christ Jesus is the one who died—more than that, who was raised—who is at the right

hand of God, who indeed is interceding for us. Who shall separate us
from the love of Christ?

And the answer to that question is, *Nothing!* Which means that all
those who belong to Christ *will* persevere. They must, and they will.
It is certain. Why? Because God is already now in Christ 100% for
us. Perseverance is not the means by which we get God to be for us;
it is the effect of the fact that God is already for us. You cannot ever
make God be for you by your good works because true Christian
good works are the fruit of God's already being for you.

"By the grace of God I am what I am, and his grace toward me
was not in vain. On the contrary, I worked harder than any of them,
though *it was not I, but the grace of God* that is with me" (1 Cor.
15:10). My hard work is not the cause but the result of blood-bought
grace. "Work out your own salvation with fear and trembling, for
it is God who works in you, both to will and to work for his good
pleasure" (Phil. 2:12–13). Working out your salvation is not the cause
but the result of God's working in us—God's being 100% for us. "I
will not venture to speak of anything except what Christ has accomplished through me" (Rom. 15:18). If we are able to do anything by
way of obedience, it is because Christ is already 100% for us.

If every exertion you make in the discipline of perseverance is a
work of God, then these exertions do not make God become 100%
for you. They are the result of his already being 100% for you. He
is for you because you are in Christ. And you cannot improve on the
perfection or the sacrifice of Christ. If by faith you are in Christ, God
is as much for you in Christ as he will ever be or could ever be. You
don't persevere to obtain this. Because of this, you *will* persevere.

So when the fear of not persevering raises its head, don't try to
overcome it by saying, "Oh, there is no danger, we don't need to
persevere." You do. There will be no salvation in the end for people
who do not fight the good fight and finish the race and keep the faith
and treasure Christ's appearing. And don't try to overcome the fear
of not persevering by trying to win God's favor by your exertions in
godliness. God's favor comes by grace alone, on the basis of Christ
alone, in union with Christ alone, through faith alone, to the glory
of God alone. He is totally, 100% irrevocably for us because of

the work of Christ if we are in Christ. And we are in Christ not by exertions but by receiving him as our sacrifice and perfection and Treasure.

Overcoming the Fear of Not Persevering

So what is the right way to overcome the fear of not persevering in old age? The key is to keep finding in Christ our highest Treasure. This is not mainly the fight to *do* but the fight to *delight*. We keep on looking away from ourselves to Christ for his blood-bought fellowship and his help. Which means we keep on believing. We keep on fighting the fight of faith by looking at Christ and valuing Christ and receiving Christ every day.

Kissing Away the Fear

Spurgeon says that God kisses away the fear of aging with his promises. Philippians 1:6: "I am sure of this, that he who began a good work in you will bring it to completion at the day of Jesus Christ." First Corinthians 1:8–9: "[He] will sustain you to the end, guiltless in the day of our Lord Jesus Christ. God is faithful, by whom you were called into the fellowship of his Son, Jesus Christ our Lord." Jude 24: "[He] is able to keep you from stumbling and to present you blameless before the presence of his glory with great joy." Romans 8:30: "Those whom he predestined he also called, and those whom he called he also justified, and those whom he justified he also glorified." No one is lost between justification and glorification. All who are justified are glorified. The point of telling us that is to kiss away all fear. If God is for us, no one can successfully be against us (Rom. 8:31).

The Key to Growing Old to God's Glory

Therefore, perseverance is necessary for final salvation, and perseverance is certain for all those who are in Christ. The works we do on the path of love do not win God's favor. They result from God's favor. Christ won God's favor. And we receive him by faith alone. And love is the overflow and demonstration of this faith.

This is the key to growing old to the glory of God. If we are going to make God look glorious in the last years of our lives, we must be satisfied in him. He must be our Treasure. And the life that we live must flow from this all-satisfying Christ. And the life that flows from the soul that lives on Jesus is a life of love and service. This is what will make Christ look great. When our hearts find their rest in Christ, we stop using other people to meet our needs, and instead we make ourselves servants to meet their needs. This is so contrary to the unregenerate human heart that it stands out as something beautiful to be followed or something convicting to be crucified.

It works both ways. Polycarp, the bishop of Smyrna, illustrates both and what it may mean for us to grow old to the glory of God.

The Perseverance of Polycarp

Polycarp was the Bishop of Smyrna in Asia Minor. He lived from about A.D. 70 to 155. He is famous for his martyrdom, which is recounted in *The Martyrdom of Polycarp*.[2] Tensions had risen between the Christians and those who venerated Caesar. The Christians were called atheists because they refused to worship any of the Roman gods and had no images or shrines of their own. At one point a mob cried out, "Away with the atheists; let search be made of Polycarp."

At a cottage outside the city, he remained in prayer and did not flee. He had a vision of a burning pillow and said to his companion, "I must needs be burned alive." The authorities sought him, and he was betrayed to them by one of his servants under torture. He came down from an upper room and talked with his accusers. "All that were present marveled at his age and constancy, and that there was so much ado about the arrest of such an old man." He asked for permission to pray before being taken away. They allowed it, and he was "so filled with the grace of God that for two hours he could not hold his peace."

In the town, the sheriff met him and took him into his carriage and tried to persuade him to deny Christ: "Now what harm is there in saying 'Lord Caesar,' and in offering incense . . . and thus saving thyself?" He answered, "I do not intend to do what you advise." Angered, they hastened him to the stadium where there was a great tumult.

---

[2]The following quotes come from this account as translated and recorded in *Documents of the Christian Church*, ed. Henry Bettenson (Oxford University Press, 1967), 9–12.

The proconsul tried again to persuade him to save himself: "Have respect to thine age . . . ! Swear by the genius of Caesar . . . Repent . . . Say, 'Away with the atheists! [that is, Christians].'" Polycarp turned to the "mob of lawless heathen in the stadium, and he waved his hand at them, and looking up to heaven he groaned and said, 'Away with the atheists.'" Again the proconsul said, "Swear, and I will release thee; curse the Christ." To this Polycarp gave his most famous response: "Eighty and six years have I served him, and he hath done me no wrong; how then can I blaspheme my king who saved me?"

The proconsul said again, "Swear by the genius of Caesar." And Polycarp answered, "If thou dost vainly imagine that I would swear by the genius of Caesar, as thou sayest, pretending not to know what I am, hear plainly that I am a Christian." The proconsul replied, "I have wild beasts; if thou repent not, I will throw thee to them." To which Polycarp replied, "Send for them. For repentance from better to worse is not a change permitted to us; but to change from cruelty to righteousness is a noble thing."

The proconsul said, "If thou doest despise the wild beasts I will make thee to be consumed by fire, if thou repent not." Polycarp answered, "Thou threatenest the fire that burns for an hour and in a little while is quenched; for thou knowest not of the fire of the judgment to come, and the fire of the eternal punishment, reserved for the ungodly. But why delayest thou? Bring what thou wilt."

The proconsul sent word that it should be proclaimed aloud to the crowd three times, "Polycarp hath confessed himself to be a Christian." After the crowd found out that there were no beasts available for the task, they cried out for him to be burned alive. The wood was gathered, and as they were about to nail his hands to the timber he said, "Let me be as I am. He that granted me to endure the fire will grant me also to remain at the pyre unmoved, without being secured with nails." The fire did not consume him, but an executioner drove a dagger into his body. "And all the multitude marveled at the great difference between the unbelievers and the elect."

When we are so satisfied in Christ that we are enabled to willingly die for him, we are freed to love the lost as never before, and Christ is shown to be a great Treasure.

A Charge to Baby Boomers

I am sixty-two years old—just about the oldest baby boomer (January 11, 1946). Behind me come seventy-eight million boomers, ages forty-four to sixty-two. Over ten thousand turn sixty every day. If you read the research, we are a self-centered generation.

> *Likes*: working from home, anti-aging supplements, climate control
> *Dislikes*: wrinkles, Millennial sleeping habits, Social Security, insecurity
> *Hobbies*: low-impact sports, uberparenting, wining and dining
> *Hangouts*: farmer's markets, tailgate parties, backyards
> *Resources*: $2.1 trillion[3]

What will it mean to get old to the glory of God as a baby boomer in America? It will mean a radical break with the mindset of our unbelieving peers. Especially a break with the typical dream of retirement. Ralph Winter is the founder of the U. S. Center for World Missions and, in his early eighties, is still traveling, speaking, and writing for the cause of Christ in world missions. He wrote an article titled "The Retirement Booby Trap" almost twenty-five years ago when he was about sixty. In it he said,

> Most men don't die of old age, they die of retirement. I read somewhere that half the men retiring in the state of New York die within two years. Save your life and you'll lose it. Just like other drugs, other psychological addictions, retirement is a virulent disease, not a blessing. . . .
>
> Where in the Bible do they see [retirement]? Did Moses retire? Did Paul retire? Peter? John? Do military officers retire in the middle of a war?[4]

Millions of Christian men and women are finishing their formal careers in their fifties and sixties, and for most of them there will be a good twenty years before their physical and mental powers fail. What will it mean to live those final years for the glory of God? How will we live them in such a way as to show that Christ is our highest Treasure?

---

[3]Accessed 9-27-07 at http://www.iconoculture.com/microsites/boomers/?gclid=COvX07OX5Y4 CFSISQQod-x1QKQ.
[4]Ralph Winter, "The Retirement Booby Trap," *Mission Frontiers* 7 (July 1985): 25.

The Perseverance of Charles Simeon

When I got prostate cancer and had surgery at age sixty, I recalled the experience of Charles Simeon and prayed that his outcome would be true for me.

Simeon was the pastor of Trinity Church, Cambridge, two hundred years ago. He learned a very painful lesson about God's attitude toward his "retirement." In 1807, after twenty-five years of ministry at Trinity Church, his health broke when he was forty-seven. He became very weak and had to take an extended leave from his labor. Handley Moule recounts the fascinating story of what God was doing in Simeon's life.

> The broken condition lasted with variations for thirteen years, till he was just sixty, and then it passed away quite suddenly and without any evident physical cause. He was on his last visit to Scotland . . . in 1819, and found himself, to his great surprise, just as he crossed the border, "almost as perceptibly renewed in strength as the woman was after she had touched the hem of our Lord's garment."
>
> He says that he had been promising himself, before he began to break down, a very active life up to sixty, and then a Sabbath evening [retirement!]; and that now he seemed to hear his Master saying: "I laid you aside, because you entertained with satisfaction the thought of resting from your labour; but now you have arrived at the very period when you had promised yourself that satisfaction, and have determined instead to spend your strength for me to the latest hour of your life, I have doubled, trebled, quadrupled your strength, that you may execute your desire on a more extended plan."[5]

How many Christians set their sights on a "Sabbath evening" of life—resting, playing, traveling, etc.—the world's substitute for heaven since the world does not believe that there will be a heaven beyond the grave. The mindset of our peers is that we must reward ourselves now in this life for the long years of our labor. Eternal rest and joy after death is an irrelevant consideration. When you don't believe in heaven to come and you are not content in the glory of Christ now, you will seek the kind of retirement that the world seeks. But what a strange reward for a Christian to set his sights on! Twenty years of leisure (!) while living in the midst of the Last Days of infinite

---

[5]Handley C. G. Moule, *Charles Simeon* (London: The Inter-Varsity Fellowship, 1948, orig. 1892), 125.

consequence for millions of people who need Christ. What a tragic way to finish the last mile before entering the presence of the King who finished his last mile so differently!

The Perseverance of J. Oswald Sanders

When I heard J. Oswald Sanders at the Trinity Evangelical Divinity School chapel speaking at the age of eighty-nine say that he had written a book a year for Christ since he was seventy, everything in me said, "O God, don't let me waste my final years! Don't let me buy the American dream of retirement—month after month of leisure and play and hobbies and putzing around in the garage and rearranging the furniture and golfing and fishing and sitting and watching television. Lord, please have mercy on me. Spare me this curse."

Passion: Making God's Greatness Known to Future Generations

That is my prayer for you as well. I close with a passion and a promise. The passion is Psalm 71:18—a passion to make the greatness of God known to the generations we are leaving behind: "Even to old age and gray hairs, O God, do not forsake me, until I proclaim your might to another generation, your power to all those to come." Oh, that God would give us a passion in our final years to spend ourselves to make him look as great as he really is—to get old to the glory of God.

Promise: We Are As Secure As Christ Is Righteous and God Is Just

The promise is from Isaiah 46:3–4: "[You] have been borne by me from before your birth, carried from the womb; even to your old age I am he, and to gray hairs I will carry you. I have made, and I will bear; I will carry and will save." Don't be afraid, Christian. You will persevere. You will make it home. Sooner than you think. Live dangerously for the One who loved you and died for you in his thirties. Don't throw your life away on the American dream of retirement. You are as secure as Christ is righteous and God is just. Don't settle for anything less than the joyful sorrows of magnifying Christ in the sacrifices of love. And then in the Last Day, you will stand and hear, "Well done, good and faithful servant. . . . Enter into the joy of your master" (Matt. 25:21, 23).

Chapter 3

Certainties That Drive Enduring Ministry

John MacArthur

When I was still a young boy, my dad reminded me of the words of the apostle Paul: "Take up the whole armor of God, that you may be able to withstand in the evil day, and having done all, to stand firm" (Eph. 6:13). Then he said something I'll never forget: "A lot of people have said and done a lot of things, but when the smoke clears, they're not all standing." And he directed me in those early years to Paul's epitaph: "I have fought the good fight, I have finished the race, I have kept the faith" (2 Tim. 4:7). Dad challenged me very early in my life to make that my goal.

Being Thankful Backwards and Forwards

My dad went to heaven in 2005 at the age of ninety-one, and into his ninety-first year he was still teaching a Bible class every Sunday. His father, my grandfather, died at a much earlier age from cancer, and I clearly remember standing by his bedside. I think I was about nine or ten, and my father said to him, "Dad, is there anything you want?" He replied, "I want to preach one more sermon." You see, he had prepared one and didn't get to preach it but was feeling like the prophet Jeremiah, who said, "There is in my heart as it were a burning fire shut up in my bones, and I am weary with holding it in, and I cannot" (Jer. 20:9). So my dad took his father's notes, printed them, and passed out the sermon at the funeral. The title of that sermon was "Heavenly Records." So my grandfather preached *on* heaven *from* heaven.

I cannot thank God enough for the legacy of such men who were faithful to the very end. Going the other direction, I am even more grateful that my four children know and love our Lord and are raising their dear ones in his nurture and admonition. Recently on a Sunday night I baptized two of my own grandchildren. I stood in the water and heard the precious testimonies of Ty and Olivia, cousins to one another and both grandchildren to me. Their parents and I could hardly contain our gratitude to God for his grace in our lives and for the blessing that Grace Community Church has been in our lives. There is nothing like the tremendous, relentless, comprehensive, and unified effort of a whole congregation of godly people bringing the truth of Scripture to bear on young lives. I delight in the one church I've been privileged to pastor for all these years, and especially for the joy of seeing my family grow in that church and be spiritually anchored there.

Wanting to Leave and Start over Somewhere Else

Many pastors move from church to church and serve numerous churches over the course of a lifetime. Sometimes the trials of ministry have almost made me wish I could do that. I'll never forget walking into a staff meeting one day many years ago where five young guys whom I had personally discipled were waiting for me. I cared for those men, having met with them in the early hours during the week to go over spiritual things, pray with them, and build them into a staff of pastors who worked alongside me. As I walked in I couldn't help saying, "I just want to tell you guys how much I love you," to which one of them responded, "If you think we're your friends, you've got another thing coming." They then tried to muster support from the rest of the staff and elders to depose me as pastor and take me out of the pulpit! They failed, but the sad fallout was that four out of the five men left the ministry for life. It was almost more than I could bear. I *would* have gone if I knew of anywhere else to go. That was about my eighth year in the pulpit at Grace.

About eighteen years in, 250 people left the church. They said my preaching was too long, too irrelevant, too dull, and a whole lot of other things. A few of those people were church elders, and that tempted me to question everything. Again I would have gone, but there wasn't anyone handing me any invitations. That was by the grace of God, however.

The Best Is Now Because . . .

I *am* grateful for all I have been through, for this is the best, the most wonderful, the most satisfying, and the most fulfilling time of my entire life. I thank God for every day he has allowed me to shepherd Grace Church. People have asked me, "How do you have such a long, enduring ministry?" From God's viewpoint, his divine, sovereign providence has worked in a myriad of ways (both known and unknown to me) that have kept me where I am. But what about from my side of things? I will tell you immediately I'm not going to present any clever insights, novel approaches, or imaginative ideas that I've managed to develop. I have no innovative technique to recommend to you. I've invented no clever strategy. I have no confidence in the schemes and strategies of men, especially when it comes to doing the Lord's work, so giving you such a program is the furthest thing from my mind.

There is only one thing I have endeavored to do, and that is *focus my entire life on biblical principles, sound doctrine, and divine truth*. While all the circumstances of life ebb and flow and the sands of human fashions shift, the foundation you want to be building on is the bedrock of God's Word. Since those early years with my dad, I have sought to be like the man in Luke's Gospel whom Jesus said built his house by digging *deep* and laying a foundation on solid rock (Luke 6:48). That doesn't happen because you *wish* it to happen, however. You can't merely speak it into existence, contrary to what some people say. As Jesus said, it's not merely coming to him and hearing his words but acting on them (Luke 6:47) that makes a person like the wise builder he described. The blessing comes not in the knowing but in the doing, as Jesus told his disciples in the upper room (John 13:17).

Paul on the Mount Everest of His Life

My dad pointed me toward one of the wisest builders of all when he cited the life and words of Paul to me in my young life. When Paul wrote in his last letter about fighting the good fight, even to the end of his days, he was at the Everest of his life, breathing the rarefied air understood only by those who not only climb to the very pinnacle but also make that climb with nobility and integrity. Paul managed to do that, even though all in Asia had forsaken him. The rest of 2 Timothy 4 indicates that his life—even at the end—was filled with its normal disappointments. There was no great crowd cheering Paul on when he reached his epic moment and finally approached the finish line. In fact, the church had largely turned their affections away from him, and the world was about to chop his head off.

Paul's Way Up Was, in a Sense, Down

Let's go back to Paul's life at the beginning of 2 Corinthians:

> Blessed be the God and Father of our Lord Jesus Christ, the Father of mercies and God of all *comfort*, who *comforts* us in all our *affliction*, so that we may be able to comfort those who are in any affliction, with the *comfort* with which we ourselves are *comforted* by God. For as we share abundantly in Christ's *sufferings*, so through Christ we share abundantly in *comfort* too. If we are *afflicted*, it is for your *comfort* and salvation; and if we are *comforted*, it is for your *comfort*, which you experience when you patiently *endure* the same *sufferings* that we suffer. Our hope for you is unshaken, for we know that as you share in our *sufferings*, you will also share in our *comfort*. For we do not want you to be ignorant, brothers, of the *affliction* we experienced in Asia. For we were so utterly burdened beyond our strength that we despaired of life itself. Indeed, we felt that we had received the *sentence of death*. But that was to make us rely not on ourselves but on God who raises the dead. (2 Cor. 1:3–9)

The comfort came because Paul's life was saturated with suffering and affliction. Everything that could come at that man came at him: physical persecution, deprivation, and illness, alongside spiritual battles and disappointments. The thematic backbone of 2 Corinthians, in fact, is a chronicle of Paul's highs and lows:

• "We are afflicted in every way, but not crushed; perplexed, but not driven to despair; persecuted, but not forsaken; struck down, but not destroyed; always carrying in the body the death of Jesus, so that the life of Jesus may also be manifested in our mortal flesh." (2 Cor. 4:8–11)

- "As servants of God we commend ourselves in every way: by great endurance, in afflictions, hardships, calamities, beatings, imprisonments, riots, labors, sleepless nights, hunger . . . dishonor . . . slander. . . . We are treated as impostors . . . having nothing." (2 Cor. 6:4–10)
- "When we came into Macedonia, our bodies had no rest, but we were afflicted at every turn—fighting without and fear within. But God, who comforts the downcast, comforted us." (2 Cor. 7:5–6)

Even the great apostle Paul suffered from depression? Yes, he did.

- "Are they servants of Christ? I am a better one—I am talking like a madman—with far greater labors, far more imprisonments, with countless beatings, and often near death. Five times I received at the hands of the Jews the forty lashes less one. Three times I was beaten with rods. Once I was stoned. Three times I was shipwrecked; a night and a day I was adrift at sea; on frequent journeys, in danger from rivers, danger from robbers, danger from my own people, danger from Gentiles, danger in the city, danger in the wilderness, danger at sea, danger from false brothers; in toil and hardship, through many a sleepless night, in hunger and thirst, often without food, in cold and exposure. And, apart from other things, there is the daily pressure on me of my anxiety for all the churches. Who is weak, and I am not weak? Who is made to fall, and I am not indignant?" (2 Cor. 11:23–29)
- "Because of the surpassing greatness of the revelations, a thorn was given me in the flesh, a messenger of Satan to harass me, to keep me from becoming conceited. Three times I pleaded with the Lord about this, that it should leave me. But he said to me, 'My grace is sufficient for you, for my power is made perfect in weakness.' Therefore I will boast all the more gladly of my weaknesses, so that the power of Christ may rest upon me. For the sake of Christ, then, I am content with weaknesses, insults, hardships, persecutions, and calamities. For when I am weak, then I am strong." (2 Cor. 12:7–10)

I just want you to see all those passages because that's the man who came to the end of his life and said, "I have fought the good fight, I have finished the race, I have kept the faith." How did Paul manage to do that? The disappointments he faced were enough to crush him. In fact, the main occasion for the writing of 2 Corinthians was that the church had turned on Paul to follow false teachers—after he had invested nearly two years of his life bringing them the knowledge of Christ! Paul knew the pain of unrequited love. Sometimes it seemed that the more he loved them, the less they loved him back! Some in the church hammered on him even for his appearance. They said his appearance was unimpressive and his speech was downright contemptible, which is to say he was ugly and couldn't communicate. Now if you're ugly but can communicate, you can make it; or if you're handsome and just stand there and talk, you can survive for a while. But the false teachers were endeavoring to take him out on every front! They wanted to discredit Paul as much as possible so they could remove the people's confidence in him and replace his teaching with their own lies.

It's hard to bear such rejection when you've poured your life into a congregation. I don't come close to having gone through all that Paul did, but I've been in one church long enough to see just about every kind of attack on my character, life, and ministry; so I've made a study of Paul's life to learn how to survive. One phrase I have camped on is, "We do not lose heart" (2 Cor. 4:16). The Greek term is *ekkakeo*, which contains the root *kak*, always a reference to evil, sin, and fallenness. This is more than just not getting discouraged or burned out; it is a commitment not to defect spiritually, whether through cowardice, laziness, immorality, indifference, or abandonment of calling and duty. But how?

Paul Embraced the Superiority of the New Covenant

First, Paul embraced with all his heart the superiority of the new covenant: "Therefore, having this ministry by the mercy of God, we do not lose heart" (2 Cor. 4:1). The ministry he was referring to is described in the previous chapter as "the ministry of the Spirit" (v. 8) and "the ministry of righteousness" (v. 9), in contrast to the "ministry of condemnation." It is the ministry of the new covenant, which the Old Testament predicted:

> Behold, the days are coming, declares the LORD, when I will make a new covenant with the house of Israel and the house of Judah, not like the covenant that I made with their fathers on the day when I took

them by the hand to bring them out of the land of Egypt, my covenant that they broke, though I was their husband, declares the LORD. But this is the covenant that I will make with the house of Israel after those days, declares the LORD: I will put my law within them, and I will write it on their hearts. And I will be their God, and they shall be my people. (Jer. 31:31–33)

That covenant is salvation in Jesus Christ. It is better because the new covenant gives *life*: God "made us competent to be ministers of a new covenant, not of the letter but of the Spirit. For the letter kills, but the Spirit gives life" (2 Cor. 3:6). The laws of Moses passed a death sentence; the gospel of Jesus Christ gives life. Paul went on to explain that although the old covenant was a "ministry of condemnation" (v. 9), it had a certain glory because it is a reflection of God's holiness. Nevertheless, the new covenant has a surpassing glory because it provides forgiveness and lasting righteousness (vv. 10–11).

It also brings *hope*, which produces *courage*. That is why Paul wrote, "Since we have such a hope, we are very bold" (v. 12).

It is *clear*, for the old was veiled, but with the new, the veil is gone (vv. 13–14).

It is *Christ-centered*, for the veil is removed "through Christ" (v. 14).

It is *empowered by the Spirit*, transforming us into the very image of the Lord from one level of glory to the next (vv. 17–18).

To know the gospel, to believe it with all your heart, and to be called to proclaim it is the most noble and exalted privilege any person could ever have! That led Paul to write:

Thanks be to God, who in Christ always leads us in triumphal procession, and through us spreads the fragrance of the knowledge of him everywhere. For we are the aroma of Christ to God among those who are being saved and among those who are perishing, to one a fragrance from death to death, to the other a fragrance from life to life. Who is sufficient for these things? (2 Cor. 2:14–16)

In spite of everything, Christ wins in the end.

If you were to ask who the most important people in a city are, you would probably hear about the mayor, the city council, and the people who run educational programs. That is *not* how God would answer the question. There's a core of people in every city who influence people for eternity. They have a profound impact on their damnation or their salvation, an aroma of death or life. Who in his own strength could have that kind of impact? Paul was stunned by the divine privilege of ministry and never lost sight of it.

My son Mark, when he was sixteen, sat down next to me and said earnestly, "Dad, when you preach, it's really something. But the rest of the time you're nothing special." He got it exactly right! He was trying to process what happened to his father when I get in the pulpit. In the pulpit what I say has divine power when I am accurately proclaiming the Word of God. At home when I have a great idea about how to fix something, it's usually stupid; but whenever someone walks up to me and says, "After I heard you preach I came to Christ," I want to step back and catch my breath. If you want to have an enduring ministry, never lose the sense of wonder and glory of the new covenant—the message the world has been waiting for. It's here, you know it, and God will use you to proclaim it. *You matter.* There's no one on this planet as powerful as the people of God, for we affect eternity.

Paul Embraced the Reality That Ministry Is a Mercy

Let's go back to 2 Corinthians 4:1, where Paul said, "Therefore, having this ministry by the mercy of God, we do not lose heart." He embraced the reality that ministry is a mercy, which is grace bestowed upon the undeserving. The godly response is gratitude, as we see from Paul's words to Timothy:

> I thank him who has given me strength, Christ Jesus our Lord, because he judged me faithful, appointing me to his service, though formerly I was a blasphemer, persecutor, and insolent opponent. But I received mercy because I had acted ignorantly in unbelief, and the grace of our Lord overflowed for me with the faith and love that are in Christ Jesus. The saying is trustworthy and deserving of full acceptance, that Christ Jesus came into the world to save sinners, of whom I am the foremost. (1 Tim. 1:12-15)

Sometimes pastors say to me, "My church isn't treating me well. I deserve to be treated better!" Really? Remember that your salvation is a mercy. The fact that you're not in hell is a mercy. Ministry itself is a mercy. People often talk about burnout in ministry, but long ago I realized that burnout is *not* because the work is too strenuous. You don't hear ditchdiggers complaining that they're getting burned out digging ditches. What makes people burn out is discouragement, and discouragement is connected to unrealistic expectations. If you realize, however, that you deserve nothing and that everything good in your life is a mercy from God, you know what you need to be able to thrive.

What happened when those 250 people walked out of the church? I was tempted to react in the flesh and say, "Those people don't appreciate me. I'm not going to take this!" and then go home to complain to my wife. The right response is, "I don't deserve to stand up and teach any of these people. If they *all* walked out next Sunday, I'd be getting what I deserve." It is a mercy I have not so affected my wife that she walked out. It is a mercy I have not somehow disappointed my children and made them turn away from Christ. It is a mercy I haven't stood in the pulpit and said such stupid things that my congregation ran me out of town!

Paul Embraced the Necessity of a Pure Heart

There is a third element I want to mention to you. Paul went on to say, "We do not lose heart. But we have renounced disgraceful, underhanded ways. We refuse to practice cunning or to tamper with God's word, but by the open statement of the truth we would commend ourselves to everyone's conscience in the sight of God" (2 Cor. 4:1–2). What is more important than holiness? "Let us cleanse ourselves from every defilement of body and spirit, bringing holiness to completion in the fear of God," Paul would write a little later on (7:1). He wanted to present the church to Christ "as a pure virgin" (11:2). "I fear," he admitted, that "I may have to mourn over many of those who sinned earlier and have not repented of the impurity, sexual immorality, and sensuality that they have practiced" (12:21). Paul wrote against all forms of sin and categorized them into useful personal checklists, which he first applied to himself. That is why he had no secret sinful life, which is particularly significant since he was an ex-Pharisee who was a master hypocrite. According to Jesus in Matthew 23, the Pharisees were whitewashed tombs full of dead men's bones; so they were masters at covering up hidden shame.

Time and truth go hand in hand: given enough time, the truth *will* come out. James explained that lust is conceived on the inside, but it soon gives birth to sin (James 1:14–15). I've spent forty years in the same congregation. Some of those dear people know everything there is to know about me upside down and backwards and about my children and grandchildren. If you're living a hidden life, it's going to come out, and you're not going to make it. The only way to avoid that problem is dealing with sins of the heart on an ongoing basis.

Paul was honestly able to state, "Our boast is this, the testimony of our conscience, that we behaved in the world with simplicity and godly sincerity, not by earthly wisdom but by the grace of God, and supremely so toward you" (2 Cor. 1:12). The conscience is not a heavenly court, but it is the highest earthly court, for it is the soul's warning system. Romans 2 explains that it either accuses or excuses us. It is to the soul what pain is to the body. Your conscience makes you feel guilty, anxious, sleepless, and filled with regret or it brings joy, affirmation, peace, and contentment.

I remember reading years ago about an Avianca airplane that flew straight into a mountain. It was a Boeing jet full of people that was on its final approach to landing. When the plane's radar detected that the plane was off course and headed for a mountain, it triggered an electronic warning voice that said, *Pull up! Pull up! Pull up!* Inexplicably, the pilot did *not* pull up. The last sound recorded on the cockpit recorder was the pilot saying, "Shut up, gringo!" just before he switched the warning system off. Less than a minute later, he hit the side of the mountain, and everyone on board perished in an instant. The radar described the reality, and the warning system reacted, but the pilot did precisely what many foolish people do with their own consciences.

God has placed inside each one of us a conscience that acts as an early-warning system. The more you saturate your conscience with the Word of God, the better informed and more useful it will be to you. That was the testimony of King David, who wrote, "I have stored up your word in my heart, that I might not sin against you" (Ps. 119:11). That was the testimony of Paul, who could say, "My conscience is clear. I'm winning the battle on the inside."

In 1749 Charles Wesley wrote a little-known hymn called "I Want a Principle Within." I think we should sing it more often as a form of self-protection:

> I want a principle within
> Of watchful, godly fear,
> A sensibility of sin,
> A pain to feel it near.
> I want the first approach to feel
> Of pride or wrong desire,
> To catch the wandering of my will
> And quench the kindling fire.
>
> From Thee that I no more may stray,
> No more Thy goodness grieve
> Grant me the filial awe, I pray
> The tender conscience give.
> Quick as the apple of an eye,
> O God, my conscience make;
> Awake my soul when sin is nigh,
> And keep it still awake.
>
> Almighty God of truth and love,
> To me Thy pow'r impart;
> The mountain from my soul remove,
> The hardness from my heart.
> Oh, may the least omission
> Pain my reawakened soul,
> And drive me to that blood again,
> Which makes the wounded whole.

Paul Embraced the Duty of Accurately Handling the Word of God

Paul explained to the Corinthian church that he and his coworkers in Christ steadfastly "renounced disgraceful, underhanded ways. We refuse to practice cunning or to tamper with God's word, but by the open statement of the truth we would commend ourselves to everyone's conscience in the sight of God" (2 Cor. 4:2). The Greek word translated "cunning" (*panourgia*) speaks of someone capable of doing anything to reach his goals by being shrewd, unscrupulous, and deceptive. There are plenty of so-called ministers like that, but all true ministers of Jesus Christ shun such manipulative techniques, following instead the example of Paul and company: "We are not, like so many, peddlers of God's word, but as men of sincerity, as commissioned by God, in the sight of God we speak in Christ" (2 Cor. 2:17). Nothing purifies a person's motives like remembering that "all [things] are naked and exposed to the eyes of him to whom we must give account" (Heb. 4:13).

Be faithful and true to the Word of God. Have a relentless commitment to biblical fidelity. If you don't do that, you can't survive long in one place. You'll have to take your show on the road or on TV, where it is easier to manipulate people since they don't get to know you day in and day out. If I manipulate a passage of Scripture for selfish ends, eventually I'm going to get caught. Rather, my commitment is to follow Paul's command to Timothy: "Do your best to present yourself to God as one approved, a worker who has no need to be ashamed, rightly handling the word of truth" (2 Tim. 2:15). That requires lots of hard work and study, but that is the minister's calling.

The truth of Scripture has an ally in a very foreign place, the human heart, "for when Gentiles, who do not have the law, by nature do what the law requires, they are a law to themselves, even though they do not have the law. They show that the work of the law is written on their hearts, while their conscience also bears witness, and their conflicting thoughts accuse or even excuse them" (Rom. 2:14–15). There is no ally in the human heart for your thoughts and ideas, but there *is* for divine truth, so be careful to handle it accurately to bring about the best results.

Paul Embraced the Truth That the Results of His Ministry Did Not Depend on Him

Paul continued, "Even if our gospel is veiled, it is veiled only to those who are perishing. In their case the god of this world has blinded the minds of the unbelievers, to keep them from seeing the light of the gospel of the glory of Christ, who is the image of God" (2 Cor. 4:3–4). Paul realized he was not ultimately in control of the results of his evangelistic ministry.

That is the same point Jesus made so well in the Parable of the Soils, which our Lord himself thought was so important. He said, "Do you not understand this parable? How then will you understand all the parables?" (Mark 4:13). The sowing of the seed reveals that there are different levels of receptivity in the soil, but if someone today representing technique-driven evangelicalism were to reinvent this parable, it would go something like this:

> There was one soil and four sowers. One sower had a particular evangelistic technique that did not go over well at all. The second sower had another evangelistic technique that did a bit of good for a while. The next one had yet another technique that also produced a superficial response. But finally came number four who had the right technique and he had thirtyfold, sixtyfold, and a hundredfold responses because it's all about technique.

But that's *not* the way Jesus told the story: He focused not on the sower but on the soil. We all sow the same seed, but only God can plow the soil.

There are serious flaws in market-driven theology. Perhaps foremost is the notion that the preacher's primary job is to overcome consumer resistance to persuade people to buy this product called Jesus. *Perish the thought!* It's bad enough that the notion is blasphemous, but it also is utterly ineffective, because the fundamental reason for consumer resistance to the gospel is much too big a problem for you or me to overcome. Let me put it this way: if I try to sell my soap to corpses in a funeral parlor, I don't think I'm going to have any buyers! I'm not exaggerating either, because Holy Scripture describes the spiritual state of unbelievers this way: "You were dead in the trespasses and sins in which you once walked, following the course of this world, following the prince of the power of the air, the spirit that is now at work in the sons of disobedience" (Eph. 2:1–2). So "if our gospel is veiled," says Paul, it is veiled to people who are in a state of destruction, compounded by the fact that "the god of this world [Satan] has blinded the minds of the unbelievers, to keep them from seeing the light of the gospel of the glory of Christ, who is the image of God" (2 Cor. 4:3–4).

Try to grasp this thought: Everything we as believers do here on earth we'll do better in heaven except for one thing, and that's evangelism, because there won't be anyone in heaven who hasn't already embraced the gospel. Evangelism is our Lord's Great Commission to us. He said to go into the whole world and preach the gospel, but then we're told that our audience is dead and blind! I am reminded of what happened to Isaiah, who saw a vision of God in heaven. God gave him a message to deliver, saying, "Go, and say to this people: 'Keep on hearing, but do not understand; keep on seeing, but do not perceive.' Make the heart of this people dull, and their ears heavy, and blind their eyes; lest they see with their eyes, and hear with their ears, and understand with their hearts, and turn and be healed." Isaiah naturally asked, "How long, O Lord?" (Isa. 6:9–11). The Lord responded that it would take awhile, and most people would be devastated, but not all, for he would establish his "holy seed" (v. 13). Salvation is a work of God. Jesus, in response to the question, "Who can be saved?" replied, "What is impossible with men is possible with God" (Luke 18:26–27).

A reporter asked me several years ago, "Do you have a great desire to build the church?" I said, "Are you kidding? Jesus said *he* would build the church. Do you think I want to compete with him?"

You don't want to spend too much time thinking about the task of evangelism from only the human perspective, but a little reflection can help us thank God for his work in salvation. This is how Paul explained it:

> The word of the cross is folly to those who are perishing, but to us who are being saved it is the power of God. For it is written, "I will destroy the wisdom of the wise, and the discernment of the discerning I will thwart." Where is the one who is wise? Where is the scribe? Where is the debater of this age? Has not God made foolish the wisdom of the world? For since, in the wisdom of God, the world did not know God through wisdom, it pleased God through the folly of what we preach to save those who believe. (1 Cor. 1:18–21, citing Isa. 29:14)

Paul goes on to tell why the gospel at first appears hard to believe to those who hear it: "Jews demand signs and Greeks seek wisdom, but we preach Christ crucified, a stumbling block to Jews and folly to Gentiles." But those whom God prompts discover that the gospel is both "the power of God and the wisdom of God." Why? "For the foolishness of God is wiser than men, and the weakness of God is stronger than men" (1 Cor. 1:22–25).

There's an etching near the Circus Maximus in Rome that's behind a metal grate so you can't touch it. I've seen it many times. It's a picture of a crucified jackass with a man's body and the head of a donkey. The translation of what's written underneath is, *Alexamenos worships his god.* That represents the scorn of the Gentile world on anyone who would dare worship a crucified man because as far as they knew, only scum ever made it to a cross. The gospel is, in a sense, an unbelievable message that is contrary to all natural inclinations, and we're trying to deliver it to people who are dead and blind. If you're not seeing people coming to Christ in droves, you know why.

To overcome those very serious problems, shall we recruit an elite crew? That is not what God did. "Consider your calling, brothers," writes Paul. "Not many of you were wise according to worldly standards, not many were powerful, not many were of noble birth. But God chose what is foolish in the world to shame the wise; God chose what is weak in the world to shame the strong; God chose what is low and despised in the world, even things that are not"—the nobodies— "to bring to nothing things that are, so that no human being might boast in the presence of God . . . so that, as it is written, 'Let the one who boasts, boast in the Lord'" (1 Cor. 1:26–31, citing Jer. 9:23). That is why Paul later wrote, "What then is Apollos? What is Paul? *Servants* through whom you believed, as the Lord assigned to each. I planted, Apollos watered, but God gave the growth. So neither he who plants nor he who waters is anything, but only God who gives the growth" (1 Cor. 3:5–7).

Let me tell you something important about that word *servants*: It literally speaks of slaves—people who were owned by someone else and had no personal rights. We in America have a built-in contempt for all forms of human slavery. And it is well that we should, given the almost unbearable agony and generations of sin that have been bred by every system of slavery that has ever existed. However, if we are going to understand how Scripture portrays what it means to be a true follower of Christ, we need to understand something of what it meant to be a slave in Roman times. Paul made the point clear in 2 Corinthians 4:5, where he described his own ministry: "What we proclaim is not ourselves, but Jesus Christ as Lord, with ourselves as your servants for Jesus' sake." The Greek term translated "servants" referred to the bottom rung in the slave chain, galley slaves who rowed the oars, for instance. While it is true that Jesus is the friend of sinners, he is also Lord and Master of all, telling his disciples:

> "Will any one of you who has a servant plowing or keeping sheep say to him when he has come in from the field, 'Come at once and recline at table'? Will he not rather say to him, 'Prepare supper for me, and dress properly, and serve me while I eat and drink, and afterward you will eat and drink'? Does he thank the servant because he did what was commanded? So you also, when you have done all that you were commanded, say, 'We are unworthy servants; we have only done what was our duty.'" (Luke 17:7–10)

The Bible doesn't condone slavery, but neither does it expressly condemn it. The New Testament *does* employ the imagery of a slave as an appropriate metaphor to picture the Christian's relationship to the Lord. We depend on him to provide for all our needs, both physical and spiritual. Even our ability to work comes from him, for the Word instructs, "You shall remember the LORD your God, for it is he who gives you power to get wealth" (Deut. 8:18). The ultimate disposition of your life regarding judgment and reward is likewise in his hands.

If you're still struggling with the biblical concept of slavery, especially because it was a part of your forefathers' past, realize that for you and me it is but a memory, but for earlier generations and for people in Bible times, it was reality. Look at these words from Philippians 2 with new eyes: "Have this mind among yourselves, which is yours in Christ Jesus, who, though he was in the form of God, did not count equality with God a thing to be grasped, but made himself nothing, taking the form of a servant [slave], being born in the likeness of men. And being found in human form, he humbled himself by becoming obedient to the point of death, even death on a cross" (vv. 5–8). If you're tempted to think it's beneath you to be a slave, remember that it wasn't beneath your Lord to be a slave. What happened as a result? God the Father "has highly exalted him and bestowed on him the name that is above every name, so that at the name of Jesus every knee should bow, in heaven and on earth and under the earth, and every tongue confess that Jesus Christ is Lord, to the glory of God the Father" (Phil. 2:9–11, citing Isa. 45:23).

Here is another triumphant conclusion from Paul: "For God, who said, 'Let light shine out of darkness,' has shone in our hearts to give the light of the knowledge of the glory of God in the face of Jesus Christ" (2 Cor. 4:6). Paul was thinking, of course, about Genesis 1:3: "God said, 'Let there be light,' and there was light." He who turned on the lights of the universe can do the same in a darkened heart by turning that heart toward Christ, in whom "the whole fullness of deity dwells bodily" (Col. 2:9).

We don't need to worry about matters of "style." That is grossly overemphasized in Christendom today, and church leaders waste untold energy fussing over whether to style their worship services as contemporary, postmodern, traditional, formal, informal, Emerging, Emergent, or country-and-western. I've been all over the world and have seen just about every possible way you can conduct a church service, but style alone doesn't mean much of anything. In fact, more often than not, too much stress on style obscures the significance of the message itself. The only way the light goes on in a person's life is if you preach the gospel of Jesus Christ. Trying to find whatever style suits the most people is folly if it's really true that "what we proclaim is not ourselves, but Jesus Christ as Lord, with ourselves as your servants [slaves] for Jesus' sake" (2 Cor. 4:5).

Paul Embraced the Reality of His Own Insignificance

I've already written about verses 5–6, but here is verse 7: "we have this treasure in jars of clay, to show that the surpassing power belongs to God and not to us." You cannot explain the impact of the gospel message by looking at those whom God has called as preachers. What a contrast: a treasure (the massive, blazing, shining, glorious gospel) in earthen vessels or clay pots (things that are cheap, common, breakable, and replaceable)! The power of the glorious gospel is not the product of human genius or technique. We are weak and common, plain and fragile, breakable and disposable, but that does not prove fatal to the work of God. On the contrary, we demonstrate that God *must* be at work, for that is the only logical explanation! Paul's humility sustained him, as it will all true servants of Christ. In contrast to our message we are nothing. When we humble ourselves in the presence of the Lord, he will exalt us (Jas. 4:10).

Paul Embraced the Benefits of Suffering

Success frightens me because it panders to my flesh. When Paul looked at his own life, he thought of himself not only as a mere clay pot but also as a battered one: "We are afflicted in every way, but not crushed; perplexed, but not driven to despair; persecuted, but not forsaken; struck down, but not destroyed" (2 Cor. 4:8-9). These four contrasts all say the same thing, which is that Paul experienced severe trials in his ministry, but none of them prevailed.

One of the greatest trials Paul experienced was his thorn in the flesh. Do you remember what Paul learned from God's own lips about that trial? The Lord said, "My grace is sufficient for you, for my power is made perfect in weakness." Paul got the message, for he responded, "Therefore I will boast all the more gladly of my weaknesses, so that the power of Christ may rest upon me. For the sake of Christ, then, I am content with weaknesses, insults, hardships, persecutions, and calamities. For when I am weak, then I am strong" (2 Cor. 12:9–10). Life is what you choose to focus on, and Paul learned to focus on the good that God could work out of even the most distressing circumstances. He could say a hearty amen to James 1:2–4: "Count it all joy, my brothers, when you meet trials of various kinds, for you know that the testing of your faith produces steadfastness. And let steadfastness have its full effect, that you may be perfect and complete, lacking in nothing." We began by considering the end of Paul's life, so we know that he is a perfect example of that principle.

The prosperity gospel is absolutely non-biblical. It is an affront to God. The way to power is through suffering and weakness. As Paul said, "For the sake of Christ . . . I am content with weaknesses, insults, hardships, persecutions, and calamities. For when I am weak, then I am strong." All true servants of Christ learn through the years to embrace the assaults that cut to the heart, the mutinies, the betrayals, the disaffection, the massive disappointment, the heartache, and even the physical pain and suffering because they know all those things work together to destroy self-reliance. Paul said, "[We are] always carrying in the body the death of Jesus, so that the life of Jesus may also be manifested in our bodies" (2 Cor. 4:10). In other words, Christ is more powerfully revealed in his servants when they bear up under severe affliction. Jesus has already died, risen, and ascended to heaven. People can't get at him anymore, but they can get to us. People will sometimes hate us for Jesus' and the gospel's sake. Paul knew all about that, saying, "I bear on my body the marks of Jesus" (Gal. 6:17) and "I rejoice in my sufferings for your sake, and in my flesh I am filling up what is lacking in Christ's afflictions for the sake of his body, that is, the church" (Col. 1:24). Can you and I say with Paul, "He took the blows meant for me, so I'll take the blows meant for him—let them come!"?

Paul spoke of death many times using the common Greek word *thanatos*, but in 2 Corinthians 4:10 he speaks about dying (*nekrosin*), not death, because he's talking about a process, not an event. He is saying, "My whole life is in the process of dying because of Christ, but it's necessary in order that the life of Jesus also may be manifested in my life." The power of God will be on display in our suffering. We all learn more, far more, from suffering. I remember when my son had a brain tumor and then my wife was in a car accident. The doctors said if she didn't die she'd be a quadriplegic. Oh, the agony of those days and hours! I gave her to the Lord in prayer many times every day, just as I had given my son to him, before those trials were so wonderfully resolved in their complete recoveries. You experience those kinds of things, and they shatter you, but they also make you stronger than before and help you sense a closer kinship with Christ.

Paul Embraced the Need for Bold Conviction

Enduring ministry does not belong to people who easily go along with the trends. I think about that when I go to Tulsa and see Oral Roberts University. The radically modernistic look of the buildings is stylized from the 1960s, and something about the campus reminds me of a parking lot for antique spacecraft! The style of architecture they chose was very forward-looking in 1965, but today it's outmoded. When you go to a university, typically what you see is classic brick, columns, and other enduring, timeless kinds of features. That's an illustration of why faddish things are best avoided. The same is true in ministry. Paul wrote, "Since we have the same spirit of faith according to what has been written, 'I believed, and so I spoke,' we also believe, and so we also speak, knowing that he who raised the Lord Jesus will raise us also with Jesus and bring us with you into his presence" (2 Cor. 4:13–14, citing Ps. 116:10). His was a ministry not driven by fads but by convictions.

The message itself never changes. You need to know the difference between what can change and what cannot change. There's integrity in having truth that you believe firmly, so that's what you speak, and you're not ashamed of it. Silence might mean comfort, acceptance, popularity, or even life. But like Martin Luther, your conscience is held captive by the Word of God. On it you stand and can do no less.

A person with deep conviction is not hunting for something to say. Rather, he is hunting for someone to say it to! I am sorry to tell you, however, that men of conviction are often unwelcome in churches today. I am thankful for the men we train at The Master's Seminary, and we send out about a hundred graduates a year. Some of the stories that come back are heartbreaking, however. Many churches don't want pastors who say, "I believed, and so I spoke." They don't want a biblical approach to life and ministry—but praise God for the churches that do! Eventually God, in his grace, finds a place for our graduates where spiritual integrity and biblical fidelity matter. We can only pray that it will matter more and more.

Paul Embraced Eternity as the Priority

Paul was so committed to the cause of Christ that his church probably cautioned him that he'd wind up dead. But Paul surely lived by the words of Jesus: "Do not fear those who kill the body but cannot kill the soul. Rather fear him who can destroy both soul and body in hell" (Matt. 10:28). He told the Corinthian church that he knew that "he who raised the Lord Jesus will raise us also with Jesus and bring us with you into his presence. For it is all for your sake, so that as grace extends to more and more people it may increase thanksgiving, to the glory of God" (2 Cor. 4:14–15). That is to say, "I will not change the message, because I believe it to be true. Therefore, I will continue to proclaim it, knowing the worst that can happen is I'm killed, but I'm going to see you in the presence of the Lord anyway. In the meantime, I'll do all I can to add one more voice to the 'Hallelujah Chorus'!"

We have eternity in view here, not comfort, popularity, or success in this life. Paul concludes:

> So we do not lose heart. Though our outer self is wasting away, our inner self is being renewed day by day. For this light momentary affliction is preparing for us an eternal weight of glory beyond all comparison, as we look not to the things that are seen but to the things that are unseen. For the things that are seen are transient, but the things that are unseen are eternal. (2 Cor. 4:16–18)

Those are staggering thoughts that come close to scraping heaven and put all our struggles into perspective. We don't lose heart in the end because we have an eternal perspective.

In view of the astounding, all-glorious reality of the new covenant, in view of the reality that ministry is a mercy that flourishes in purity and is effective only by the sovereign power of God in response to the preaching of the Word, even in the lowliest clay pot battered and bruised in the struggle, Paul embraced the perfecting power of suffering. He remained faithful to his convictions no matter the cost. His motto was, "To me to live is Christ, and to die is gain" (Phil. 1:21), for he was confident of his own resurrection and eternal reward. His focus was always on heaven, preferring the spiritual over the physical (2 Cor. 4:16), the future over the present (v. 17), and the invisible over the visible (v. 18). He kept his eye on the prize, which is an eternal weight of glory far beyond all comparison (v. 17). Nothing that can come our way in this world can compare with the magnificence of the glory that will be granted to us in the presence of our Lord.

Chapter 4

Cumulative Daily Decisions, Courage in a Cause, and a Life of Endurance

Randy Alcorn

Paul prayed that Christians might be "strengthened with all power according to [God's] glorious might, so that you may have great endurance and patience with joy, giving thanks to the Father" (Col. 1:11–12).

We're called to a life of endurance empowered by Christ, and accompanied by joyful thanksgiving. Endurance requires patience, because reward for today's right choices will come, but it may be months or years from now, or not until we leave this world. Those who drum their fingers waiting for the microwave to finish demonstrate that patient endurance doesn't come naturally.

Paul challenged his disciple, "Share in suffering as a good soldier of Christ Jesus" (2 Tim. 2:3). Soldiers expect hardship and are trained to face it. As comrades locking arms in the service of our Commander, Christ's humble warriors are to live out, on enemy-occupied territory, what Eugene Peterson called "a long obedience in the same direction."[1]

Today's roadblocks and distractions make endurance in the Christian life seem unattainable. Our temptations aren't worse than those in first-century Corinth. But televisions, computers, and even cell phones bring into our homes what used to be found only in back

---

[1]Eugene H. Peterson, *A Long Obedience in the Same Direction: Discipleship in an Instant Society*, 20th anniversary edition (Downers Grove, IL: InterVarsity Press, 2000).

alleys. In our technological Corinth, temptations are only a keypad or mouse click away.

Failure to endure—in marriage, jobs, church, or any part of life—has become normal. A consistent long-term obedience, without periodic diversions into sin and unfruitfulness, seems an impossible dream. Sin has become so common, so expected, that holy believers are either elevated as heroes or dismissed as legalists.

In our disposable society, we use something up, then toss it (whether a paper plate, a spouse, a church, or a career). The stick-to-it philosophy is a relic of another age—something monks once did, but we can't. And why should we? Who wants to work hard or become bored by staying a course when endless alternatives call to us?

But the essence of the Christian life cannot change with culture. Paul's words to the Colossians and Timothy are words to us. We should not shrink from hardship. We should endure it with patience and thanksgiving. We are to follow Christ from start to finish, repenting quickly of our sins and moving forward in deeper devotion. Yes, there will be dry times, but overall, the arc of spiritual growth will steadily rise higher, not trail off so our lives end in a wasted whimper.

Endurance is Christ's call to follow him, to finish strong for God's glory. There is no higher calling, no bigger privilege, no greater joy.

Reunion with Those Who Endure

Nanci and I attended a thirty-year reunion of our church college group. Forty came. Five from our original group had died. Most of those present had lost a parent or two; some had lost spouses, siblings, or children. A few marriages had died; two people had suffered mental breakdowns, others financial meltdowns. Some had children on drugs and in jail; several had cancer and other illnesses.

Yet it was a beautiful evening. Person after person kept saying, "God has been faithful." We lingered late, tears wondrously mixed with laughter.

We sang our old Scripture songs from the early 1970s. Instead of being disillusioned because they hadn't panned out, we were encouraged because they'd proven truer than we'd realized back then. God had indeed been "our refuge and our strength, a very present help in trouble" (Ps. 46:1). We had learned—some from great hardship—that God alone can bear the full weight of our trust. Admitting our imperfections, we experienced together the sweet fragrance of perseverance and spoke of anticipating a better world.

Understandably, some old friends couldn't come, due to distance, health, and schedule conflicts. But some didn't come because their love for Christ had grown cold. They had not endured. Why? The question could be answered different ways. My answer for our purposes is this: *their hour-to-hour and day-to-day choices set them up for spiritual distraction and failure.*

Nanci and I walked away that night with a renewed commitment to finish our lives well. I pray that you will live the years ahead so that when you receive an invitation to your reunion, you'll want to come and hear—and share—what God has done. Don't make a series of choices that will make you into the person who wants to stay away.

Endurance in a Cause

At the editors' request, I will share my personal story of perseverance in a cause. Please understand that I don't consider myself a hero. On the contrary, I am humbled by and deeply grateful for God's sustaining grace.

I grew up in a non-Christian home. When I came to Christ as a teenager, Tozer, Schaeffer, Lewis, and Bonhoeffer mentored me through their books. In 1977 I became a pastor of a new church. In the early 1980s I joined the board of the first Crisis Pregnancy Center in the Northwest, in Portland, Oregon. Nanci and I opened our home to a pregnant teenage girl and helped her place her child for adoption. We had the joy of seeing her come to faith in Christ. To this day she remains a dear friend, a courageous spokesperson for unborn children.

As the years went on God increasingly laid on our hearts the plight of the unborn. (If you don't understand who unborn children are, what follows won't make sense to you. See my book *Why Prolife?*[2] or abortion-related articles at www.epm.org; or consult www.abort73.com.)

---

[2]Randy Alcorn, *Why Prolife? Caring for the Unborn and Their Mothers* (Sisters, OR: Multnomah, 2004).

I read Scripture that said, "Rescue from death those being led to slaughter" (Prov. 24:11). And, "Speak up for those who cannot speak for themselves . . . defend the rights of the poor and needy" (Prov. 31:8–9, NIV). I couldn't escape Pastor Dietrich Bonhoeffer's courage: publicly criticizing Hitler, and calling upon the German church to stand up for the Jews. Francis Schaeffer's call to defend the unborn affected me profoundly.

In January 1989, knowing it would greatly complicate my life and my pastoral ministry, I began participating in peaceful, nonviolent civil disobedience at abortion clinics. Hundreds of pastors across the country did the same.

I went to jail for a few days, just long enough to experience my first taste of dehumanization. For instance, a jail nurse assumed I was lying about being an insulin-dependent diabetic. She refused access to my medical equipment, which had been confiscated at my arrest. When she heard why I'd been arrested she said, "Tell me you're a rapist or a murderer, but don't tell me you're one of those anti-abortionists, because that makes me *mad*." Disgusted with my insistence that I had a medical condition, she actually threw a handful of supplies at me.

Throughout my life at home, in school, and in sports, I was accustomed to being believed by those in authority. My wife, children, and church trusted me. Suddenly, behind locked doors with criminals, I was the object of distrust and derision.

On another occasion a judge sentenced me to two days in jail. I was put in chains from wrists to ankles, while cameras flashed all around me. I was pushed and shoved and taken to jail, and then strip-searched with two dozen naked men. A leering guard mocked and made sadistic comments to some of the men.

It was just a hint of what some people, guilty and innocent, have experienced. But I have never forgotten it. Though it was the most dehumanizing two days of my life, I wouldn't trade it for anything. It paled in comparison to the suffering of Jesus and of unborn children. But it was enough to make a permanent impression, giving me a reference point to the sufferings of others (and helping me to write of the persecuted church, as in my novel *Safely Home*).

An abortion clinic won a court judgment against me and a few dozen others. We'd been sued for $2,800, the cost to the clinic of the ten abortions we prevented one day. We were also held liable for the abortion clinic's attorneys' fees—another $19,000. I told a judge I would pay anybody anything I owed them, but I would not hand money to people who would use it to kill babies.

In April 1990 my church received a court order demanding that every month they send a fourth of my wages to the abortion clinic. To keep the church from having to decide between paying an abortion clinic and defying the court, I resigned.

The only way I could avoid garnishment was to make no more than minimum wage. Fortunately, our family had been living on only a portion of my church salary, and we'd recently made our final house payment, so we were out of debt. God led us to start Eternal Perspective Ministries. To this day we continue to be part of our church, though I could no longer serve as a pastor.

Endurance as a Family Decision

In February 1991, nearly two years after I resigned from the church, we were set for a major courtroom trial. Given the political climate, it seemed almost certain that we would lose this case, lose our house, and because of financial constraints have to remove our girls from the Christian school they loved.

The night before the trial, my attorney called with amazing news: "Randy, I just received a fax from the abortion clinic. They want to drop you from the lawsuit."

Incredible. Suddenly the house was no longer in jeopardy. The girls could continue in school. We'd be saved the burden, tension, and spotlight glare. "But . . . why would they drop me?" I asked the attorney.

"I figure it's because you are a pastor and a writer, so you get a lot of press. You've been explaining why you feel compelled to stand up for unborn children. Maybe they think they're better off without you. But because they've dropped you at the last minute, you have to agree. Obviously you should, considering what's at stake."

I sat down with my wife and my daughters who were then nine and eleven years old. They'd been praying right along with us, and they'd watched from across the street one time when I was arrested.

(Nanci and I believed that if we sheltered our children from life's difficulties, we would rob them of the opportunity to see God at work,
rob them of the privilege of praying, and rob ourselves of experiencing the benefits of their childlike prayers.)

I explained to Nanci and the girls what the lawyer said, then
asked, "What do you think we should do?" Karina, our eleven-year-
old, replied, "Daddy, if the abortion clinic thinks they'll be better off
without you on the case, I think God wants you there." Nine-year-old
Angela instantly agreed.

"Remember, if we lose the case—and we probably will—we could
lose our house, and we might not be able to afford your school." They
understood perfectly. As much as Nanci and I wanted to climb out of
the pressure cooker, we agreed with our daughters. We prayed about
it together over the next hour. Then I called the lawyer and floored
him by saying, "We've decided to stay on the lawsuit."

Four weeks in court followed, where we witnessed an amazing
series of false accusations. We saw clinic employees testify that we
screamed at women, grabbed them, spit on them, and called them
sluts and whores. We watched the judge—who made clear to the jury
how hostile he was toward us—read the newspaper while we were
testifying. He literally screamed at a pastor who had observed one
event and was quietly testifying as a character witness. (If someone
else had told me, I wouldn't have believed it, but I was there.)

The judge ordered a directed verdict, telling the jury they must
find us guilty and should impose upon us a judgment so large that
we would never do this again. Though there was no violence and no
property destruction, it was the largest judgment on record against
a group of peaceful protestors: $8.2 million. I used to joke that $8.2
million was more than I made as a pastor in an entire year!

Prior to being sued I had divested myself of all ownership of
everything from house and cars to bank accounts and book royalties.
Though we have never failed to pay anyone else all that they're due,
by God's grace we have never handed money to an abortion clinic. I
continue not to own any assets, and my minimum-wage salary pre-
vents the abortionists from taking anything.

Needless to say, many don't agree with our strategy, but we
believe it is the only God-honoring course of action, in light of the

alternatives. This situation brought controversy and complications to our lives, but God taught us to trust him and be patient, for which we are profoundly grateful.

To Endure, Love Jesus More Than the Cause

One thing I've learned about endurance in a cause is: *don't be primarily motivated by anger.* Yes, there is such a thing as righteous anger. God is furious about the mistreatment of the poor and needy and defenseless. But our "righteous anger" is too often self-righteous anger. Whether you are fighting human-rights violations, slavery, prostitution, pornography, drugs, crime, drunk driving, or abortion, keep your eyes on Jesus or you will either burn out or rely upon your own strength, not his. By God's grace, we never lashed out at abortion clinic personnel. My wife weekly stood outside the clinic and talked with several staff members, including the manager, sharing the love of Christ.

There's significant wear and tear upon those called to pro-life work, jail ministry, street ministry, helping the poor, aiding substance abusers and those with sexual addictions, and fighting pornography.

If you're going to endure, you must have a passion for Jesus that's bigger than your passion for the cause. Otherwise, even if you don't burn out, your cause will take the place of your Lord, thereby becoming an idol.

Lose yourself. Not in a righteous cause but in a righteous God who calls us to a variety of causes and sustains us wherever he calls us. Don't be a single-issue Christian. Chuck Colson's heart is huge for prison ministry, but much more. Joni Eareckson Tada cares deeply about the disabled, but she cares about far more. Chuck and Joni love Jesus, and that love wells up in ministries to prisoners and the disabled. That's how you find staying power in a cause—seeing that it isn't an isolated issue. It's part of the larger scheme of God's kingdom work.

If your life is centered on being against abortion or pornography or homosexual marriage, that isn't enough. William Wilberforce didn't just oppose slavery. He was in love with Jesus, and it was Jesus who sustained him through the abolition of the slave trade. It was Jesus he thanked three days before his death, when he heard the news from the House of Commons that all remaining slaves in Britain and her colonies had been declared free.

To endure in a cause, keep reminding yourself it's about Jesus: "The King will answer them, 'Truly I say to you, as you did it for one of the least of these brothers, you did it to me'" (Matt. 25:40).

And if it's not about Jesus, why is it your cause?

Families Grow through Enduring Hardship

I also learned that endurance in a cause can help build the character, faith, and insight of children. Early on we determined that though we would never sacrifice our children, we would sacrifice with our children. As I said, our children were willing to lose the only house they'd ever lived in and the school they loved. Given the outcome of the trial, it appeared they would.

As it turned out, God intervened, and we lost neither house nor school. I know God has rewarded my daughters for their willingness to sacrifice for the cause of Christ and the unborn. Instead of tearing our family apart, it knitted us together. Well-meaning people warned us that our children would suffer due to my choices. But we believed children suffer not when their parents do God's will, but when they don't.

Our children benefited in other ways, some of them difficult. When they were pre-teens, they stood with us one day across from an abortion clinic, holding large intrauterine pictures of living pre-born children. A limousine drove by slowly, then the back window came down, four feet in front of us. Out shot a man's arm, making an obscene gesture. The surprise came when we saw the man's face. It was the current mayor of Portland. No kidding. We had quite a family discussion about darkness in the human heart, including the hearts of some leaders.

Another day our daughters attended a rescue with their mother and saw all that happened, including my arrest. The next morning I read the newspaper's account of the story. I handed it to my daughter Karina, who read every word. Stunned, she started crying. "Dad, this isn't true. I was there the whole time. That's not what happened!"

Nothing I'd said to my children about the world's lies and media distortions compared to the firsthand lesson learned from the newspaper that day. Those little girls today are the godly mothers of our grandchildren. Had they not been part of the cause with us, they might never have learned many lessons that served them well and helped them begin a long obedience in the same direction.

To Endure, Consent to Being Unpopular

If you are not willing to be misunderstood and vilified, you won't endure in any worthwhile cause. I was speaking to a group of pastors in 1990 when one of them raised his hand and asked, "Why do you go to abortion clinics and scream at women and spit on them and pull their hair?" When I told him I'd never done such a thing, and never would, I asked him, "Why would you believe the newspapers instead of coming to me as your brother in Christ and asking if it's true?"

If you insist on being respected and praised, in society or in the church, you will walk away not only from the cause but from your Lord. Jesus said, "No servant is greater than his master. If they persecuted me, they will persecute you also" (John 15:20). Who are we to expect the world to treat us better than it treated Jesus? *Followers of Jesus should expect injustice and misrepresentation*, and we dare not be preoccupied with our rights and reputations.

When false testimony was given against us in court, a key verse for me was 1 Peter 2:23, which says of Jesus: "When he was reviled, he did not revile in return; when he suffered, he did not threaten but continued entrusting himself to him who judges justly." When I found myself misjudged by both unbelievers and believers, I found peace in knowing that God is my judge. Given my failings, that thought had not encouraged me before, but suddenly it did!

Nanci and I learned to have thicker skin when it came to people's disapproval. One of the greatest enemies of a long obedience in the same direction is the desire to be popular, whether with the world or the church. If your eyes are on anyone but Jesus, you're not going to have the stamina to put up with criticism. Jesus said, "If the world hates you, you know that it has hated me before it hated you" (John 15:18). There's great freedom in being able to accept that some people will never like you because your beliefs offend them. You can talk with them and pray for them, without craving or needing their approval.

Paul said, "If I were still trying to please men, I would not be a servant of Christ" (Gal. 1:10). Jesus is the Audience of One. We will stand before his judgment seat, no one else's. We should long to hear him say, "Well done, good and faithful servant." Live for the approval of others and you will not live for Christ's approval, and therefore you will not endure.

To Endure, Trust God to Bring Good out of Adversity

In our lawsuits and having to leave pastoral ministry, what the abortion clinics intended for evil, God intended for good (Gen. 50:20). Some of that was evident at the time, but much became evident as years went by. (How many years had passed before Joseph clearly saw God's purpose in his adversity?)

We saw innumerable amazing stories come out of the lawsuits. For instance, God opened a door for me to share the gospel with a prominent lesbian and abortion activist. She later came to faith in Christ. I remember a man surrendering to Jesus outside the clinic doors, and two abortion clinic employees walking away from their jobs when it dawned on them what they were doing.

For a variety of reasons, it has been seventeen years since I last engaged in civil disobedience. Endurance in a cause does not mean that you must always do the same thing. The cause was and is unborn children, not a particular strategy. I believe God called me to one method for a period of time, just as he called me to work with pregnancy centers years before that. Now we give substantial funds to support the pro-life cause. I still speak up for the unborn in messages, writings, and personal conversations. I applaud those who have spent most of their lives in this and other righteous but unpopular causes, doing far more than I have. May they joyfully endure, to God's glory.

One other fruit of the trials God took us through was that I surrendered ownership of my book royalties. Through our ministry, 100% of these royalties goes to God's kingdom: missions, famine relief, pro-life work, and aid to the disabled, prisoners, and persecuted Christians. Shortly after we gave all the royalties to the Lord, my books were suddenly on the best-seller lists. Royalties increased dramatically, as if God was saying "now that the books belong to me I'm going to really use them." Our ministry has been able to give away several million dollars as a direct result of those events that some considered terrible and tragic. Looking back, we're deeply grateful it all happened.

Some time ago, the ten-year judgment from the abortion clinic expired. Our ministry board told Nanci and me that they wanted to grant us the future royalties, which they felt we'd earned. Nanci and I talked and prayed about it. God had faithfully provided for us during the previous ten years and graciously allowed us to support great causes through the royalties. So why would we want to change that arrangement? We didn't need a higher standard of living. With joy in our hearts, we said, "No thanks."

Months later the abortion clinic got the judgment extended for another ten years. We'll always be grateful we didn't know that would happen when we made our decision. What we learned through the original trial still serves us well today. God has given us an indescribable joy in knowing that every dollar of royalties made from my books is being invested in eternity.

Endurance Takes More Than Sincere Desire

In the final analysis, endurance will be a measure of the kind of character and integrity we develop. The remainder of this chapter applies to all believers in the cause of Christ, not just to those particular causes.

I asked a gathering of thousands, "How many of you, in five or ten or thirty years from now, want to be sold out to Jesus Christ, a disciple of the King, empowered by the Holy Spirit, saturated in his Word, and yielded to his will?"

Ninety percent of the hands shot up. They meant it. Then I told them the bad news: many who raised their hands would never become that person. They would not finish well. It's easier to raise a hand today than to make the kinds of choices day after day after day that result in a long obedience in the same direction.

Every day we are becoming someone—the question is, who? Author Jerry Bridges, hearing me address this, told me that Dawson Trotman, founder of The Navigators, used to say, "You are going to be what you are now becoming."

Scripture speaks of this process of character development: "And we all, with unveiled face, beholding the glory of the Lord, are being transformed into the same image from one degree of glory to another" (2 Cor. 3:18).

You become like what you choose to behold. Behold Christ, you become Christlike. Gaze upon superficiality and immorality, and it's equally predictable what you'll become.

Who you become will be the cumulative result of the daily choices you make. "The path of the righteous is like the first light of dawn, which shines brighter and brighter until day" (Prov. 4:18). This is why Scripture continually warns us against wrong choices: "Do not enter the path of the wicked and do not walk in the way of the evil. Avoid it; do not go on it; turn away from it and pass on your way" (Prov. 4:14–15).

Our choices flow out of our hearts, and therefore we must take care to guard them from contamination: "Above all else, guard your heart, for it is the wellspring of life" (Prov. 4:23, NIV). What's the most effective way to contaminate a water supply? Poison it at its source. If you don't guard your heart from the world's values, you will be conformed to the world (Rom. 12:1–2). It takes no more effort to be conformed to the world than it does to float downstream. To be transformed by the renewing of our minds is to swim upstream against the current. Renewing our minds requires conscious, deliberate effort.

You will become the product of what you choose to delight in and meditate upon. Psalm 1 is a powerful formula for endurance: "Blessed is the man who walks not in the counsel of the wicked, nor stands in the way of sinners, nor sits in the seat of scoffers. But his delight is in the law of the LORD, and on his law he meditates day and night."

We all meditate, and we're all shaped by the object of our meditation. We take our attitudinal and behavioral cues from it. This week, will I be shaped by situation comedies, soap operas, and newspapers, or will I be shaped by Isaiah, Luke, A. W. Tozer, and Charles Haddon Spurgeon? It depends on how I choose to spend my time.

Psalm 1 says the one who continually meditates on God's Word "is like a tree planted by streams of water, that yields its fruit in its season and its leaf does not wither." Trees don't choose where to place themselves, but we do. We determine what our sources of nourishment will be, which in turn determine whether we bear fruit or wither.

Endurance Is Never Automatic

Following Christ isn't magic. It requires repeated actions on our part, which develop into habits and life disciplines.

Christ-centered endurance doesn't just happen, any more than running a marathon or climbing a mountain just happens or having a good marriage just happens.

Endurance requires a good plan, with clear and tangible steps that are taken one after the other. The farmer tills the soil. The weeds have to be removed. He doesn't say, "Lord, please remove the weeds." He prays, "Lord, give me your strength as I pull these weeds today."

The athlete doesn't say, "Lord, go out there and win that race." He says, "God, empower me to run hard and do my best, and if you so desire it, to win."

The key to spirituality is the development of little habits, such as Bible reading and memorization and prayer. In putting one foot in front of the other day after day, we become the kind of person who grows and endures rather than withers and dies.

Ten years from now, would you like to look back at your life, after you've made consistently good decisions about eating right and exercising regularly? Sure. But there's a huge gap between wishes and reality. The bridge over the gap is self-control, a fruit of the Spirit (Gal. 5:22–23). The key to self-control is discipline, which produces a long-term track record of small choices in which we yield to God's Spirit, resulting in new habits and lifestyles. Spirit-control and self-control are interrelated in Scripture, because godly self-control is a yielding of self to God's Spirit.

Most of us know the difference between eating cottage cheese and Krispy Kremes. Or the difference between a daily workout and spending life on a couch. Likewise, there's a difference between whether you read the Bible or you don't, whether you spend the evening watching *American Idol* or *Survivor* or reading the Bible or a great Christian book. While the difference today may seem small, the cumulative difference will be great.

Many people say they want to write a book. What they really

want is to *have written* a book. Talking about writing a book is very easy. Writing a book is very difficult. That's why there are more talkers than writers. And that's why more people talk about the Christian life than live it.

We want the fruit of the spiritual disciplines, but often we're unwilling to do the work they actually require. We want the rewards without the sacrifices.

One of my favorite websites for young people is www.TheRebelution.com, directed by Alex and Brett Harris. They challenge young people to "Do Hard Things" (the title of their first book).[3] They're saying, "Let's not be a generation of self-centered materialists; let's discipline ourselves to follow Jesus and do hard things to his glory."

The life of endurance requires us doing many hard things. But these hard things are the very ones that bring purpose, joy, and satisfaction to our lives.

Endurance Involves Daily Choices to Do Good Works

I know what some readers are thinking right now. *Doesn't this emphasis on cultivating discipline in the Christian life sound legalistic, an attempt at works-righteousness? We shouldn't be talking about works, just grace, right?*

Wrong. While the Reformers opposed works-righteousness, they *never* opposed righteous works. Indeed, God honored a multitude of righteous works, and a spirit of disciplined endurance, to bring about the Reformation. It is God's sovereign grace that empowers us to do good works, which are central to our calling:

> For by grace you have been saved through faith. And this not from your own doing; it is the gift of God, not as a result of works, so that no one may boast. For we are his workmanship, created in Christ Jesus for good works, which God prepared beforehand, that we should walk in them. (Eph. 2:8–10)

Notice that this text doesn't say God has prepared doctrines for us to believe, but works for us to do. He has a lifetime of good works laid

---

[3] Alex Harris and Brett Harris, *Do Hard Things: A Teenage Rebellion against Low Expectations* (Colorado Springs: Multnomah Books, 2008).

out for us. We are not saved *by* good works, but we are saved *to do* good works by his power and to his glory.

Scripture frequently depicts God's empowerment of us alongside our effort to live out the empowered Christian life: "Him we proclaim, admonishing everyone and teaching everyone . . . that we may present everyone mature in Christ. For to this end I toil, struggling with all his energy that he so powerfully works within me" (Col. 1:28–29).

So, if you wish to persevere, ask God to empower you to put one foot in front of the other. Then start moving your feet. When the alarm goes off in the morning, ask God for strength. But don't ask him to levitate you out of bed, flip the Bible open, and turn the pages for you.

Endurance Means Keeping Discipline's Purpose in Front of Us

In *Spiritual Disciplines of the Christian Life*[4] Donald Whitney tells the story of six-year-old Kevin, whose parents enrolled him in music lessons. After school every afternoon, he sits dejectedly in the living room and strums a guitar while watching his buddies across the street play baseball.

One day Kevin is visited by an angel, who takes him to Carnegie Hall. Kevin witnesses onstage a great guitar player. Kevin's awed by the man's skill and the beauty of his performance. Finally the angel asks, "What do you think, Kevin?" His answer is, "Wow!"

Suddenly they're back in Kevin's living room. The angel tells him, "The wonderful musician you saw is *you* in another fifteen years." Then he adds, "But only if you practice!"

Kevin is energized. Now he has a vision, a purpose for his daily disciplines. Practice can still be hard, but it's worthwhile because he sees its purpose, he sees what it will make him into.

"Discipline yourself for the purpose of godliness" (1 Tim. 4:7, NASB). The Greek word for discipline here means to exercise.

Exercise isn't glorious, any more than guitar practice is glorious. I help coach high school tennis. We're constantly working on things

---

[4]Donald S. Whitney, *Spiritual Disciplines of the Christian Life* (Colorado Springs: NavPress, 1991).

in practice that will help us in competition. Teams that don't practice don't win. Athletes who don't practice don't excel or endure in their sport.

Whenever I'm tempted not to exercise, which is often, I remind myself of the *purpose* of exercise, the end result, and the rewards it brings. Also, the consequences of *not* exercising. I do the same with the spiritual disciplines, rehearsing their purpose and results, as well as the consequences of not doing them. This motivates me.

When was the last time you spent time with God, studied Scripture, or read a great book and later regretted it? Why do we neglect what most enriches us and brings us joy and contentment?

If you don't have the purpose of that discipline clear in your mind, you'll turn off the alarm and stay in bed. If you're determined to start the day with God, you'll have to drag your body out of bed. There's no such thing as *spiritual* disciplines without the *physical* disciplines that make them possible.

> Do you not know that in a race all the runners run, but only one receives the prize? So run that you may obtain it. Every athlete exercises self-control in all things. They do it to receive a perishable wreath, but we an imperishable. So I do not run aimlessly; I do not box as one beating the air. But I discipline my body and keep it under control, lest after preaching to others I myself should be disqualified. (1 Cor. 9:24–27)

After telling Timothy he should endure hardship as a good soldier, Paul says, "An athlete is not crowned unless he competes according to the rules. It is the hardworking farmer who ought to have the first share of the crops" (2 Tim. 2:3–7).

What do soldiers, athletes, and farmers have in common? They all take physical action. They are disciplined. They are deliberate. They work hard. Only then do they enjoy the pleasure of victory and harvest. Without hard work, no Christian will endure.

Dallas Willard says in *The Spirit of the Disciplines*:

> It is part of the misguided and whimsical condition of humankind that we so devoutly believe in the power of effort-at-the-moment-of-action alone to accomplish what we want and completely ignore the need for character change in our lives as a whole. The general failing

is to want what is right and important but at the same time not to commit to the kind of life that will produce the action we know to be right and the condition we want to enjoy. This is the feature of human character that explains why the road to hell is paved with good intentions. We intend what is right, but we avoid the life that would make it a reality.[5]

Offering Our Bodies for the Life of Endurance

Endurance requires a lifetime of yielding your body to the Holy Spirit.

Do not let sin reign in your mortal body so that you obey its evil desires. Do not *offer* the parts of your body to sin, as instruments of wickedness, but rather *offer* yourselves to God . . . and *offer* the parts of your body to him as instruments of righteousness. (Rom. 6:12–14, NIV)

What can we do without our bodies? That's the significance of Romans 12:1–2:

I urge you, brothers, in view of God's mercy, to offer your bodies as living sacrifices, holy and pleasing to God—this is your spiritual act of worship. Do not conform any longer to the pattern of this world, but be transformed by the renewing of your mind. (NIV)

Notice the interrelation of mind and body. It's not just that we should renew our minds and expect that our bodies will follow. Rather, we offer our bodies to place ourselves where our minds can be renewed.

We use our hands to write the check and put it in the offering plate. Where we put our treasure through the physical discipline of giving, our hearts will follow (Matt. 6:21).

We open our mouths to share the gospel. We move our legs to run from immorality. We avert our eyes to avoid looking at someone with lust.

Bodily actions open a Bible and turn off a television. To read a book or listen to God we have to make a concerted effort to turn our ears and eyes away from this loud, invasive world.

---

[5]Dallas Willard, *The Spirit of the Disciplines: Understanding How God Changes Lives* (New York: HarperCollins, 1991), 6.

We're not only spiritual beings, we're physical. If we don't offer our bodies as living sacrifices, our minds won't be renewed. Why? Because our minds will only be fed and shaped by the input our bodies provide them.

Consider again Psalm 1. "Blessed is the man who walks not in the counsel of the wicked, nor stands in the way of sinners, nor sits in the seat of scoffers. But his delight is in the law of the LORD, and on his law he meditates day and night." In each case, there is a physical action—walk, stand, sit. To meditate on the Word involves opening it with our hands, looking at it with our eyes, or speaking it with our lips.

"Look carefully then how you walk, not as unwise but as wise, making the best use of the time" (Eph. 5:15–16). Why not redeem two hours of your day that you would have spent on television, newspaper, video games, phone, working overtime, or hobbies? Change your habits. Spend one hour meditating on and/or memorizing Scripture. Spend the other hour reading a great book. Share what you're learning with your spouse and children, or a friend.

Listen to Scripture and audio books and praise music while you fold clothes, pull weeds, or drive. Say no to talk radio or sports radio, not because they're bad but because you have something better to do. Fast from television, radio, and the Internet for a week. Discover how much more time you have. Redeem that time by establishing new habits of cultivating your inner life and learning to abide in Christ. "I am the vine; you are the branches. Whoever abides in me and I in him, he it is that bears much fruit; for apart from me you can do nothing" (John 15:5).

Give Jesus first place in your life. Don't just let your life happen, choose what to do with it, or in the end you'll wonder where it went. If you're going to persevere as Christ's follower, you must consciously choose not to squander your life or let it idle away, but to invest it in what matters.

Choosing Companions for the Life of Endurance

You will become the kind of person you choose to spend time with, whether at work or school or church or the coffee shop. "Do not be misled: 'Bad company corrupts good morals'" (1 Cor. 15:33).

Talk to those who've endured, and you'll find they've chosen good friends who raise the bar instead of lowering it. Make sure your friendships are centered on Christ. If your closest friends don't follow Jesus, you'll have all kinds of daily reasons not to follow him. If they do follow Jesus, positive peer pressure will hold you accountable to the life of discipleship. "He who walks with the wise grows wise, but a companion of fools suffers harm" (Prov. 13:20). Whom we choose to spend our leisure time with will dramatically shape our lives.

Television and reading both put us in someone's company, and remove us from someone else's company. You decide: will you be different because you put yourself in the company of Spurgeon rather than Seinfeld? Over the long haul, will you grow closer to God and your family and your neighbor by watching television, or by turning it off and doing something that matters, something that's an investment in eternity?

A great way to endure in the Christian life is to study and pattern your life after followers of Jesus who have lived a long obedience in the same direction. To do this, you must read history and biographies. Take your cues from dead people who still live rather than the living who are dead. Compare reading a biography of William Wilberforce or Amy Carmichael to watching *The Simpsons* or a sitcom. Which will help you grow in Christlikeness? Take your eyes off celebrities and put them on followers of Jesus. Ask yourself, what did they do to become who they became, and how can I arrange my life to follow their example?

You needn't read just about pastors or theologians. Stanley Tam is a businessman who declared God to be the owner of his company, U.S. Plastic. R. G. Letourneau, the inventor of earth-moving machines, gave 90% of his salary to God.

God has also placed in your church examples of a long obedience in the same direction. Find them and spend time with them. Sit at the feet of the wise, not fools.

Bad books are poor companions; good books are great friends. I've just finished rereading Bonhoeffer's *The Cost of Discipleship*. This morning I was reading C. S. Lewis, and his fingerprints are still on me this afternoon. I enjoy good movies and a limited amount of television. But the fact is, had I spent the day watching television, I wouldn't have progressed in a life of discipleship.

That's why I'm deeply concerned about the plummeting literacy rate, especially among young men. Increasingly, boys spend their time on video games, movies, television, websites, iPods, and phones that have everything from text messaging to Internet to television. They are reading significantly less than boys of previous generations. Boys who don't read become men who don't read. If someone's not a reader, he's not a reader of God's Word. Unless this trend is reversed—which will not happen without decisive intervention—it will result in a tide of unrighteous thinking and living, as well as a vast crisis of leadership in tomorrow's church.

We are in serious danger of losing coming generations to shallowness, immorality, and heresy because they are not digging deep into Scripture and great books grounded in Scripture. Families and churches who are committed to building Christian character that will endure must address this problem head-on.

Enduring by Anticipating Our True Country

> But according to his promise we are waiting for new heavens and a new earth in which righteousness dwells. (2 Pet. 3:13)

> He was looking forward to the city that has foundations, whose designer and builder is God . . . they were strangers and exiles on the earth . . . seeking a homeland . . . they desire a better country, that is, a heavenly one. Therefore God is not ashamed to be called their God, for he has prepared for them a city. (Heb. 11:10, 13–16)

These passages speak of looking forward to our home in heaven. On the New Earth as resurrected people we'll forever dwell with our Lord Jesus, reigning over God's creation as he first intended. Yet many Christians are *not* looking forward to this. They are looking forward to no more than promotion or retirement. With such unworthy and short-term dreams, they cannot endure the hardships of discipleship or enjoy its pleasures.

Consider how hardship looks from an eternal perspective:

> The sufferings of this present time are not worth comparing with the glory that is to be *revealed in us*. For the creation waits with eager

> longing for the revelation of the sons of God . . . the creation itself will be set free from its bondage to corruption. (Rom. 8:19)

> For this light and momentary affliction is preparing for us an eternal weight of glory beyond all comparison, as we look not to the things that are seen but to the things that are unseen. (2 Cor. 4:17–18)

One day we'll be with the Person we were made for, living in the Place we were made for. Joy will be the air we breathe. We will be forever grateful there for the persevering grace extended to us by Jesus, King of kings.

We should remind ourselves regularly that the best is yet to be. We have yet to reach our peaks, and when we reach them in the resurrection, we will never pass them. This assurance will help us here and now live self-controlled and disciplined lives of deferred gratification, knowing that eternal rewards await us in the presence of our Lord, the Headwaters of Eternal Joy.

Humility, Generosity, and Purity as Paths to Endurance

> Clothe yourselves . . . with humility toward one another, for "God opposes the proud but gives grace to the humble." Humble yourselves, therefore, under the mighty hand of God so that at the proper time he may exalt you. (1 Pet. 5:5–6)

Choose pride and you get God's opposition. Choose humility and you get God's grace. This is why the proud fall away while the humble endure. It's why none of us should ever view ourselves as celebrities, only servants. We are God's errand boys and girls. And what a privilege that is!

God humbles us in the ways he knows best. Two of the best things God ever did for me were to give me a chronic disease (insulin-dependent diabetes), and abortion-clinic lawsuits that forced me to resign as pastor of the church I loved. I wouldn't have chosen either, but I'd gladly take both rather than give up what I've learned about trusting God. Through our thorns in the flesh God says, "My grace is sufficient for you, for my power is made perfect in weakness."

"Pride goes before destruction, and a haughty spirit before a fall" (Prov. 16:18). Perhaps the two greatest ways God takes down the proud are the two greatest threats to endurance in the Christian life: our culture's twin idols of Money and Sex.

The Idol of Money

Jesus warns about being choked by "the deceitfulness of riches" (Matt. 13:20–22). Wealth promises what it never delivers: fulfillment, contentment, joy. Things have mass, and mass has gravity, and gravity puts people in orbit around things. They become our center instead of Christ.

Those deceived by the health-and-wealth gospel often fall away when illness, suffering, and poverty strike. They imagine God has broken his promises, because they've ignored promises such as "all who desire to live a godly life in Christ Jesus will be persecuted" (2 Tim. 3:12). Christians around the world know suffering and glorify God in their suffering, enduring to the end. Prosperity theology, entitlement theology, is not from Jesus—it's the creation of Christianized western materialism. Any gospel that is truer in California than in China is not the true gospel.

As I address in my books *The Treasure Principle* and *Money, Possessions and Eternity*, giving is the only antidote to materialism. One of the best ways to persevere in your faith is to give away more, leaving yourself with fewer vested interests in what distracts you from Christ and more in what draws you to him. As Jesus said, "where your treasure is, there your heart will be also" (Matt. 6:21).

So why not determine a finish line of what you and your family need to live on and give away the rest to God's Kingdom? What you keep will not satisfy you; what you give will loosen Money's hold on you and help you experience the grip of Christ's grace.

We know the prayer warriors in our churches. Where are the giving warriors? Where does the next generation look to be mentored in giving? How can we expect them to live lives of Christian perseverance when they have learned from us to be Christian materialists?

The Idol of Sex

Sexual immorality is the other great deterrent to enduring in the Christian life. Countless Christians, including church leaders, have been shipwrecked through one unwise choice after another that leads eventually to moral ruin. Those who imagine they're not in danger of being robbed will leave cash out in plain sight and fail to lock the door. Those who think sexual immorality won't happen to them likewise make unwise choices in where they go and what they do and with whom they spend time that virtually guarantee it will.

Satan has targeted us for immorality, and society provides no end of ammunition. Tragically, even most Christian homes provide access to it. Christian parents must stop being naive and start protecting their children. If you have a teenage boy with Internet access in his room, you might as well fill his closet with hundreds of pornographic magazines and say, "Don't look at them." If that seems harsh, you don't understand how many young men, including those in the church, are becoming enslaved to pornography in their own homes. (And how many Christian girls are visiting chat rooms and flirting with men.)

A lasting legacy of Christ-centeredness cannot be left by those captive to lust. When we allow our children access to pornography, chat rooms, and much of what's found on MySpace, as well as television and movies saturated with immorality, we are undermining anything they are learning about Jesus. These things pull them away from Jesus, never toward him.

If we and they are to endure in the Christian life, we must topple the Sex idol and guard our hearts, giving ourselves to Jesus anew each day, each hour. Only then will we be set free from the bondage to sin that now dominates popular culture. Only then will we be able to protect our children. Certainly we will never succeed in guiding them and guarding them from what is enslaving us.

Conclusion: The Elliot Brother You Don't Know

January 2006 was the fiftieth anniversary of the death of the five missionaries martyred in Ecuador. That month in our church services I interviewed Steve Saint, son of Nate Saint, and Mincaye, one of the tribal warriors who killed the missionaries and later came to faith in Christ. One of Ed McCully's sons joined us when we were invited by Jim Elliot's family to have dinner in Portland at the house Jim grew up in.

There we were, with family members of three of the five martyrs, along with Mincaye, who is like family to them now. Also with us were Jim Elliot's older brother, Bert, and his wife, Colleen. In 1949, when Bert and Colleen were students at Multnomah Bible College, they were invited to Peru by a missionary. They became missionaries to Peru years before Jim went to Ecuador.

That January when we met them they were on a furlough. When we were talking about Peru, Bert smiled and said, "I can't wait to get back." Now in their eighties, they're nearing their sixtieth year as missionaries. Until that weekend I didn't know anything about these people. Bert and Colleen Elliot will enter God's Kingdom "under the radar" of the church at large, but not under God's.

Bert said something to me that day I'll never forget: "Jim and I both served Christ, but differently. Jim was a great meteor, streaking through the sky."

Bert didn't finish by describing himself. But I'll describe him this way: a faint star that rises night after night and faithfully crosses the same path in the sky, unnoticed on earth.

Unlike his brother Jim, the shooting star.

I believe Jim Elliot is experiencing great reward. But I wouldn't be surprised to one day discover that Bert and Colleen Elliot's reward is even greater.

> Multitudes that sleep in the dust of the earth will awake: some to everlasting life, others to shame and everlasting contempt. Those who are wise will shine like the brightness of the heavens, and those who lead many to righteousness, like the stars forever and ever. (Dan. 12:2–3, NIV)

Bert and Colleen Elliot have lived a long obedience in the same direction. Whether we follow God to leave our country or to stay here, all of us are likewise called to a life of faithful endurance, empowered by Christ.

Wouldn't it be great to get to the end of our lives with as few regrets as possible?

So let's ask ourselves, *when our life here is over, what will we wish we'd done less of and more of?*

In terms of character-building choices, why not ask God to empower you to spend the rest of your life closing the gap between what you'll wish you would have done and what you really have done?

Chapter 5

One Thing

Helen Roseveare

The subject the authors of this book were asked to address was "A Call for the *Endurance* of the Saints." I slightly changed this in my own thinking to "A Call for the *Perseverance* of the Saints." In England the word *endurance* has a connotation of gritting your teeth, keeping a stiff upper lip, and getting through the job in hand somehow. But the word *perseverance* makes one think of steadily going on and refusing to give up, no matter what comes.

Caleb

When I began thinking about the subject, my mind went very quickly to Caleb. Caleb was *eighty-five* years old when he reminded Joshua of a promise that Moses had made to him to "give me this mountain" (KJV) when they reached the Promised Land. I read Caleb's story again, first in Numbers 13–14 and then in Deuteronomy 1:36 and then particularly in Joshua 14. Five times we read a telling phrase in the context of Caleb—"*wholly followed*" (Num. 32:12; Deut. 1:36; Josh. 14:8, 9, 14). He followed the Lord wholeheartedly. There was nothing halfhearted about him. There was no sometimes on, sometimes off, sometimes hot, sometimes cold. There was no choosing when he would follow or when he wouldn't. And he was eighty-five years old! I'm not quite there yet, but I thought, *that* is what I want to be like—wholehearted.

Somebody recently asked me, "Who are your heroes?" I had to stop and think. *I really don't have any heroes except Jesus.* But I realize that in one sense, Caleb is one of my heroes. He was still going strong at eighty-

five years of age, still prepared to fight for a mountain that was inhabited
by giants with fortified cities. He went for it. He did not give up.

Polycarp

Then I thought of Polycarp, the Bishop of Smyrna. He was *eighty-six* years old when he was burned at the stake in A.D. 156. He could
have saved his life, had he cursed Christ. But he said, "Eighty and six
years have I served him, and he has done me no wrong; how then can
I blaspheme my king who saved me?"[1]

Blandina

Next I thought of Blandina, a slave girl—fragile in body, timid in
mind. She was subjected to every kind of torture during the first
century, yet she could not be compelled to deny her faith before they
ultimately butchered her to death. So age is of no account: a young
slave and a bishop at the end of his life—both were sold out to following Jesus to the end.

Hebrews 12

That takes us easily into Hebrews 12:1, where we are commanded to
throw off everything that hinders—to throw off the sin that so easily
entangles—and to "run with *perseverance*" (NIV) the race marked out
for us. This race is not only for Caleb or Bishop Polycarp or Blandina
but also for each one of us. All of us who know and love our Lord
Jesus are to run with perseverance the race marked out for us, fixing
our eyes on Jesus.

In February 2006 a Bible teacher in my country, the Rev. Edward
Lobb, preached two sermons in my home church on Hebrews 12. He
stressed the fact that as Christians we are not called to a picnic. We're
not given a hammock when we enter our fifties or sixties. We're not
invited to put our feet up and say it's done. No. That's just not the
way it is. We are called to a race, which needs determination, guts,
and endurance to finish. Anyone can start a race, but what matters is
getting to the end.

---

[1]For more on Polycarp's remarkable courage and perseverance, see John Piper's chapter in this
book.

The writer to the Hebrews was writing to persecuted Jewish Christians. They were persecuted to the extent of being turned out of the temple. They'd lost all that had been dear to them through Old Testament days—temple worship, all the fine clothing of the high priest, and all the ordinances they had practiced. They were not even allowed to enter the temple courtyard. Suddenly they felt they'd lost an awful lot and they weren't sure what they'd gained. The writer to the Hebrews keeps on saying, "With Jesus, it's better! With Jesus, it's better! Don't seek to worship angels. Jesus is better than angels. Don't hang onto the worship practiced by the Old Testament saints. Jesus is better." He stresses this all the way through the letter, and he pleads with them not to turn away, not to shrink back or give up.

Then in chapter 11 of Hebrews we read that wonderful great list of Old Testament saints. They all stuck it out. They finished their courses, some through terrible sufferings. The writer tells us how some of them were sawn asunder, but all of them stuck it out to the end. They didn't give in, and God did not fail them or let them down.

Then in Hebrews 12:2 we read that Jesus, our great High Priest, finished the course. He finished the race that God had given to him, which was to die on the cross for you and for me. He got to the end. Remember how he cried out on the cross, "It is finished!" (John 19:30). Jesus didn't stop before he finished the job that God had given him to save you and me. He said to God, "Not my will, but yours, be done" (Luke 22:42).

Friends, you and I can finish too if we keep our eyes on Jesus and if we accept his loving discipline and endure hardships without complaining and without becoming embittered.

This past summer at a camp for teenage girls, I was giving three Bible studies on the life of David. We studied together how David was anointed as the future king and how he proved himself in the battle against Goliath. We looked at all his faithfulness in so many different directions. And then, toward the end of his reign, we read the story of Bathsheba. God graciously sent Nathan to him, and David repented. As a result of that, we have Psalm 51, and we have all the encouragement for our own hearts that if we truly repent of sin, God will forgive us. Thank God for that, yes. But why was there failure? And so near the end?

I remember an occasion at Nebobongo, the small hospital I worked at in the heart of the forestlands of northeast Congo. A youngster arrived one day—I think he was probably around eleven years old—to say that his father, who was an evangelist, was very ill out in a village way back in the forest. I was very new in Africa, and I didn't know the way. I asked the youngster, "Can you take me to him?" "Oh, yes," he replied. So I asked, "How far is it?" I knew that we had little gasoline left for the ambulance. He said, "It's two sleeps." (In other words, it had taken three days to walk to me, sleeping twice en route.) I worked out it would be roughly ninety miles, and I thought quickly, *Well, I've just about enough gasoline to get me there.* So when the boy assured me that if we could get to his father's village, they had a 400-liter drum of gasoline and would be able to fill my car up for the return trip, we set off together. He sat beside me in the cab, and we talked. Oh, good talk. I was talking about our Lord Jesus. We shared together, and I was telling him stories about Jesus. As we drove along we came to a fork in the road, and he would say, "Go right," so I went right. We came to a crossroads, and we turned, and I went on talking to him. Suddenly the car spluttered, coughed, and came to a halt. I looked at the gas gauge—we'd run out of gasoline. The boy looked around. "Doctor," he said, "I don't know where we are. I've never been here before."

We had to leave the vehicle on the side of the road and set off to walk back the way we had just come. After about two to three miles, we came to a fork. "Oh," he said, "we should have gone left here." We hadn't! We had turned right. We walked along for another two miles. It was about five miles from where I left the vehicle to where the lad's village was. We had been so near, but at the last minute we had taken the wrong fork.

It can be like that in our Christian life. It's so essential to keep going *to the end*. To start a race is fine, but it's much more important to keep going until we hit the tape.

Christ's Perseverance with Us

When I was thinking about our perseverance in following Jesus, I paused for a moment as I thought that there is actually something much more wonderful than that: it is *his* perseverance in dealing with us—you and me. I never cease to wonder at God's patience and long-suffering with me. Particularly when I'm at the Lord's Table in church, and there's a moment during the service when together we confess our sins to God, and I look back to the last time I was at the Lord's Supper, and I think, *It's the same things that I confessed last time.* It's the same impatience or irritability or being a bit sorry for myself, a pity-little-me syndrome. Once again I tell God I'm sorry and that with all my heart I really want to change. I really want God to make me more like Jesus. I *want* to be Christlike, but I fail so often. He's so patient, isn't he? He doesn't throw us off. He doesn't say, "You've had all the chances you're going to have; I'm finished with you." God is always so gracious. His perseverance with us—in transforming us into the likeness of his Son as members of his family—is amazing.

I think of a chorus that I sang when I was first saved.

Turn your eyes upon Jesus.
Look full in His wonderful face.
And the things of earth will grow strangely dim
In the light of His glory and grace.[2]

So just for a minute, before we think about our perseverance in following him, let us pause in order not to forget his perseverance with us—with you and with me.

One Thing

Every year between Christmas Day and New Year's Day I seek to have time alone with God and to ask him for a particular verse for the coming year. For 2006 he gave me a phrase out of Ephesians 1:17: *"that [I] may know him better"* (NIV). That has been the longing of my heart all year. When Paul wrote that phrase, he was at the end of his life, imprisoned in Rome. He'd been a missionary for years. He'd been serving God with all his heart for years, and yet still this prayer came out of his heart: "that [I] may know him better."

I asked the Lord for a verse for 2007, and he gave me Psalm 27:4: "One thing I ask of the LORD, this is what I seek, that I may dwell in the house of the LORD all the days of my life, to gaze upon the beauty

---

[2]Helen H. Lemmel, "Turn Your Eyes Upon Jesus" (1922).

of the LORD and to seek him in his temple" (NIV). When I was praying through this verse, one little phrase struck me straightaway. The
verse starts off with the two words, "one thing." So I looked up in
the concordance all the verses in the Bible where it says "one thing,"
and I let my mind dwell on that phrase.

I want us to think about three verses that say "one thing":
• One thing I know (a *past* fact)
• One thing I do (a *present* activity)
• One thing I seek after (a *future* aspiration)

These three point to the past, the present, and the future testimony of my Christian life.

One Thing I Know

"One thing I . . . know" comes from John 9:25. There was a man
who was born blind, and Jesus healed him. The Pharisees were saying, "Who did it?" They were arguing with the man that he wasn't
the man who'd been born blind, and if he was, then who had healed
him? The man said, "Whether he [that is, Jesus] is a sinner or not, I do
not know. One thing I do know. I was blind but now I see!" And that
was fact—actually, past fact! I pray that for every single one of us this
is a past fact in our personal experience. There was a moment when,
having been blind to the things of God, suddenly I could see!

I'll never forget that wonderful evening, the first of January, a
lovely New Year's Day over sixty years ago. I can remember it now as
though it was yesterday. I don't know how God does such wonders,
but I suddenly knew with absolute assurance that God knew me and
loved me so much that he sent his Son Jesus to die for *me*. I'd heard
this wonderful gospel throughout my first term at the university, when
I'd been going to Christian Union meetings. I don't even know why I
went to those meetings, except that they drew me, they attracted me;
but I didn't know the Savior. There was now a growing hunger in my
heart. During the Christmas holidays, the C.U. girls had arranged for
me to go to a Christian house party, and suddenly, on the last night
of the house party, I knew. *I knew that I had been blind, but now I
could see.* And this complete certainty, the knowledge of what Jesus
had done for me in the past, made me utterly sure that I was saved.

There's a teaching seeping into even what we call the evangelical

Christian church that is belittling the fact that *Jesus died for my sins*. They say that he died only as an example or some such thing. I don't honestly know how they explain away the fact of his penal death on the cross as our Savior or what they actually believe instead of the Truth. In fact, I don't know how they can call themselves Christians if they don't believe that "Jesus died for my sins." For me, that's *the* basic fact of Christianity. Jesus died for my sins. And this to me is solid *fact*. And whatever else happens in anyone's Christian life, whatever the problems or difficulties, this one thing is certain:

> Jesus my Lord will love me forever,
> From him no pow'r of evil can sever,
> He gave his life to ransom my soul;
> Now I belong to him.
> Now I belong to Jesus. Jesus belongs to me.
> Not for the years of time alone,
> But for eternity.[3]

I tend to say that on that night sixty years ago I fell in love with Jesus. I'm just overwhelmed by the fact of his love for me. The lady in charge of the house party where I was saved gave me a new Bible. The man who'd been leading the Bible studies—Dr. Graham Scroggie, a great Bible teacher in the UK during the first half of the last century—wrote a verse from Philippians in my new Bible, Philippians 3:10: "that I may know him, and the power of his resurrection, and the fellowship of his sufferings, being made conformable unto him in his death" (KJV). And then, within half an hour of having been saved, Dr. Scroggie signed me up for a four-year Bible correspondence course! It was through his tutoring, as he mentored me through those four years, that not only did I fall in love with Jesus, but I fell also in love with his Word.

When I went up to bed that night, I tried to find Philippians 3 and to read the verse in context. I knew nothing about the Bible; in fact, I was terribly ignorant of anything to do with spiritual things. I had no idea who this man Paul was who had written the chapter, but I just knew as I read the chapter that I wanted to love Jesus as he did. I wanted to love him wholeheartedly. I wanted to love him with

---

[3]Norman J. Clayton, "Now I Belong to Jesus" (1966).

all I had—to put him first in everything. That is partly why Caleb
became a pattern for me in my life—to love the Lord and to follow
him *wholeheartedly*. As I started Bible study daily, I came to verses
like Romans 8:1, "There is therefore now no condemnation for those
who are in Christ Jesus." And, "There is no other name under heaven
given among men by which we must be saved" (Acts 4:12). There is
only Jesus. He is our unique, lovely, beautiful Savior.

I went back to college, where I finished my training as a doctor.
I was accepted into our mission, WEC International. In 1953 I sailed
for Congo. All those early years at college and the first twelve years
in Congo as a missionary and then the five months of the rebellion
(civil war in Congo in 1964)—it was out of all the experiences of
those years that I was persuaded (when I had been rescued and came
home) to write my first book, trying to express this longing to love
the Lord and serve him wholeheartedly. Caleb had said, "Give me
this mountain" (Josh. 14:12, KJV). All those first years on the mission
field I longed for mountaintop experiences. I wanted to be up there. I
wanted to be seeing Jesus. I wanted almost desperately to be pleasing
to him, possibly to show him in some small way how much I loved
him. There were lots of struggles. There were moments when I was
frustrated. There were moments when I nearly gave up. I anguished
over my own failure to be what I knew God wanted me to be. But
through it all there was this great longing to love him and follow him
wholeheartedly.

One Thing I Do

Now we will consider the second "one thing." In Philippians 3:13
Paul writes, "I do not consider that I have made it my own. But one
thing I do . . ." "One thing I do" is in the present tense—the present-
active tense. "One thing I am doing. Forgetting what is behind, straining to what is ahead, I am pressing on toward the goal to win the prize
for which God has called me." Hosea 6:3 says, "Keep on keeping on."
That is a literal translation from my Swahili Bible—"Keep on keeping
on." Don't give up; rather, follow on to know the Lord to the end.
Jesus said, "You will be hated by all for my name's sake. But the one
who endures to the end will be saved" (Matt. 10:22). We know we are
his ambassadors. We've been entrusted with the word of reconcilia-

tion and are called to tell others that Jesus died for their sins. And that is *the* certainty of what should be our present-tense activity. That's what we've been sent to do. God has sent us out to tell others about Jesus. There should be an earnestness in our spirits. There should be the pressure that I must—not I may, not perhaps; it's not an optional extra—I *must* share Jesus with others. I must tell them. That's what Paul said. "One thing I do: Forgetting what's behind and straining toward what is ahead, I press on toward the goal to win the prize for which God has called me" (Phil. 3:13–14, NIV).

Even when discouragements come or a feeling of weariness or of growing older, keep going! Don't give up. We have to continue steadfast daily with *To please him* as our motto. Pleasing him in everything—in every choice that has to be made: the petty little choices, as well as every great, large choice. It doesn't matter what the choices, let our motto be: *In everything to please him.* This should be our commitment for life.

I spent a lot of my time in recent years with university students, mostly Christians, mostly trying to encourage them. Sometimes I go back to a place for a second visit, possibly a couple of years later. I may ask them, "How many of you were here when I was here last year?" They can be quite excited to put their hands up. They are rather glad to tell me they were there the last time I came. "Well," I say, "you shouldn't be here now! If you'd listened to what I'd said last time you'd now be on the mission field"—or at least in training for the next move in that direction!

There is always this temptation to slacken off, to tone down. It's easy to seek greener pastures. Somehow it's easy to think, *If only I didn't have to work with So-and-So. If only I could be in such and such a place I could be what God wants me to be. I could make a go of it, but* . . . We blame our circumstances or we blame our companion or we even blame our homes. If you're a missionary, you blame the committee. (I used to think the only reason we had committees on mission fields was so missionaries had someone to blame!) But in fact, the responsibility rests on me. The blame culture of today leads me to seek to justify myself if I'm slacking off, if I'm slowing down, if I get to a place where I say, "I can't do any more, Lord. I've done my share; I want to slow down." If I find myself thinking or talking like that, I'm in danger. We have to be 100 percent committed right through to the end.

One of the major problems I had was in learning to live a consistent Christian life wherever God put me. I spent twenty years in Congo in Central Africa, where in many ways it was very easy to be a Christian—I was the only pale-skin among some eighty thousand dark-skinned people. Wherever I went, I was immediately known as the missionary. When Africans met me they would say, "If you're a missionary, your job is talking about Jesus: so get on with it and talk about Jesus!" It was relatively easy. Then the Lord called me back to live and work in the UK. I now live just outside Belfast. I love Africans. I loved being a missionary in the middle of Africa. But I found it much harder to love affluent Westerners. In Africa, if you are walking along a jungle pathway, through the marshlands, and crossing over a narrow bridge made of slippery poles, and you meet an African coming toward you, you know that one of you has to turn back—and I couldn't! I could only just balance on those bridges; as for passing anybody, there wasn't a hope. I'd fall into the muddy waters for sure. So the other person would go backwards very graciously. I would go across to the other side and then say to him, "Do you know my best friend?" He says, "Who?" I say, "Jesus." "No," he says. "Can I introduce you to him?" "Yes," he says. And we sit down on the grassy bank, and we talk for two, three, maybe four hours. He is in no hurry. To him time doesn't matter. Now in the UK you can't do that! I haven't found it so easy there. But I've had to learn that it doesn't matter to God where he puts us. We have to learn to be consistent Christians and 100 percent in love with Jesus and fully committed to our deepest desire to be pleasing to him at all times, no matter where he places us.

That demands that we come down into the valleys. We cannot fulfill God's purpose for our lives up on the mountaintop. The disciples saw the transfigured Jesus in all his glory and radiance on the mountaintop. His garments were shining; his eyes were shining. They were in the very presence of the glory of God. Then they came down into the valley, where there was a crowd. In the crowd was a father with his epileptic (or demonized) son. That was where the work was done. The mountaintop was the place of the vision, but the work was done down in the valley. So it is for us: it's being willing to stick it out in the valley that really counts. Sometimes the valley can be very dark. It can be very lonely. It can be quite frustrating. Sometimes I felt like crying out, like that father did, "I believe; help my unbelief!" (Mark 9:24). But we have to stick at it.

During the five months that we were held by guerrilla soldiers during the Congo Civil War, there was no use in moaning and groaning about our fears and pains. I knew I was there because God had put me there. So whatever would happen to me was God's responsibility. We were ultimately rescued and were brought home to recover. Then we went back again, and people said, "Oh, aren't you wonderful!" Honestly, I wasn't particularly wonderful at all. All my adult life I'd lived out there in Congo. I'd never done medicine anywhere but in Congo. The Congolese were my family. I loved them. I didn't want to stay at home in the UK. There was truthfully nothing very wonderful about our decision to return. An urgent desire "to please Jesus" had become part of me. I truly wanted to live for him 100 percent. We had known—even when we were captives, even when the beatings were savage, even when things were unpleasant—that God was still on the throne and had not forgotten his own. He was with us. And he will be with us whatever happens. He's working out his purposes.

As I was meditating on the fact that we must share Jesus with others—anywhere, whatever the circumstances—I was reminded of two passages in Scripture. Isaiah 52:7 says, "How beautiful upon the mountains are the feet of him who brings good news, who publishes peace, who brings good news of happiness, who publishes salvation, who says to Zion, 'Your God reigns.'" Isn't that lovely? Jesus is saying to you and me, "If you're busy telling others about me, you're beautiful." Maybe no one else thinks you or I are particularly beautiful, but God says, "If you're busy telling others about Jesus, you are beautiful in my eyes."

Another passage where Jesus said that what was done was a beautiful thing was in Simon's house, at the meal table, when the woman came and broke the alabaster jar of precious ointment, anointing him, as he said, in preparation for his burial. The other disciples were grumbling: "Why this waste of perfume? It could have been sold for more than a year's wages and the money given to the poor." Jesus said, "Why do you trouble her? . . . She has done a *beautiful* thing to me" (Mark 14:4–6). That means that as we worship Jesus—pouring out our innermost soul to him, thanking him for his grace that allows us to worship him in every part of our lives, putting Jesus first, loving him, wanting to know him better, being with him—he says that is beautiful! In our service, as in our worship, God says that is beautiful. It is such condescension on God's part to consider anything that we seek to do for him beautiful, when he looks at us and says we're beautiful when we're talking to others about him.

Perhaps you know this hymn,

> My goal is God Himself, not joy nor peace,
> Nor even blessing, but Himself, my God.
> 'Tis His to lead me there, not mine but His.
> At any cost, dear Lord, by any road.
>
> One thing I know. I cannot say Him nay.
> One thing I do, I press towards my Lord,
> My God, my Glory here from day to day.
> And in the glory there, my *Great Reward*.[4]

I find that very lovely—it expresses my innermost desires toward God himself.

One Thing I Ask

That brings me to my third "one thing." It is found in Psalm 27:4. "One thing have I asked of the LORD, that will I seek after: that I may dwell in the house of the LORD all the days of my life, to gaze upon the beauty of the LORD and to inquire in his temple."

Follow this prayer with the command of Jesus to seek first his kingdom and his righteousness and his promise that all the other necessary things would be given to us as well (Matt. 6:33). My yearning in my own heart as I look forward is to have the right priorities all the time to please him in everything I do. It is my priority first and foremost to please my lovely Lord Jesus—to seek him so as to love him above all and everything else. And that's what the psalmist said— to *dwell* and to *gaze*.

---

[4]Fredrick Brook, "My Goal Is God Himself," date unknown.

Do I honestly take time to dwell with the Lord? Not as a visitor, not as a passing guest, but to dwell, to live in his temple. To live in his presence—to have nothing in my life that is not in the presence of the Lord. Have we really let him so into our lives that everything from now on that we do is done in the presence of Jesus with him as our companion?

Remember Mary and Martha. The one was busy and harassed. She just had too much to do. The other sister was sitting at the feet of Jesus, just being with him. And Jesus declared that what Mary was doing was "good" (Luke 10:42). (He doesn't actually say "better" as it reads in some translations.) What she was doing was good. "Martha, Martha," the Lord said, "you are worried and upset about many things, but only one thing is needed. Mary has chosen what is good, and it will not be taken away from her" (NIV). Do I choose what is good? Do we treasure that early hour in his presence, that quiet time alone with the Lord? It's so essential to being what he wants us to be. It's the only way we're going to become more like our lovely Lord Jesus. Can that early hour be squeezed out? Now I know that for the mothers of small children it can be very difficult to keep that quiet time. I'm well aware it may not be possible in the early hour. But we can all find some time when we can be alone with God. He will enable us to find that time if our hearts are set on it. Do I guard that time against all intrusions?

Do I love to read his Word and soak in it, more than any of the other newspapers, magazines, or whatever else? Is God's Word honestly precious to me? We'll become like Jesus more by reading the Word than by reading the daily newspaper!

Do I hunger for the feast that he's prepared for me daily? Am I hungry and thirsty after righteousness, to be holy with his holiness? Am I more quickly aware of and ashamed of failure than I was a year ago? If I'm growing more like Jesus, I will be. I will more quickly say, "I'm sorry, Lord. I shouldn't have done that or said that." Or "I should have done that or said that." I shall be more quickly sensitive to his leading me to repent. Is he beautiful in my eyes and in my heart? Do I want his beauty to rest on me? I love Psalm 90:17: "Let the beauty of the LORD our God rest upon us" (KJV). That's the beauty of his character. Think of Galatians 5:22–23: "The fruit of the Spirit is love, joy, peace, patience, kindness, goodness, faithfulness, gentleness, self-control." That's the loveliness of Jesus. Is that seen in me?

In private, in our homes, that can be much more demanding. It's what our closest family members think of us, not just the people who see us when we stand on the platform, that counts. When we are is on the platform, everybody may think we are marvelous! But it's when we are at home with people who know us well that the true test comes. Am I, are you, really revealing the loveliness of the Lord Jesus?

> Let the beauty of Jesus be seen in me,
> All his wondrous compassion and purity.
> O thou Spirit divine, all my nature refine
> Till the beauty of Jesus be seen in me.[5]

Do I long to gaze on his beauty so that I may reflect him? In that wonderful verse, 2 Corinthians 3:18, Paul says we are to be mirrors reflecting the loveliness, the glory, the beauty of Jesus, so that others looking at us will see him. Is that really happening? Is that really an expression that describes me?

Some of my favorite verses are in 1 John 3, the first three verses. "See what kind of love the Father has given to us, that we should be called children of God. . . . Beloved, we are God's children now, and what we will be has not yet appeared; but we know that when he appears we shall be like him, because we shall see him as he is," the all-together lovely One. That is beautiful. And that is what the psalmist said in Psalm 27:4: ". . . that I may dwell in the house of the LORD . . . to gaze upon the beauty of the LORD." So my life, my lips, my actions, my motivations, my reactions to other people should all reflect the loveliness of the Lord Jesus. There is a hymn that says it all:

> May *the mind of Christ* my Savior
> Live in me from day to day,
> By His love and power controlling
> All I do and say.
>
> May *the Word of God* dwell richly
> In my heart from hour to hour,

---

[5] Albert Orsborn, "Let the Beauty of Jesus Be Seen in Me." Orsborn was General of the Salvation Army (1946–1952).

So that all may see I triumph
Only through His power.

May *the peace of God* my Father
Rule my life in everything,
That I may be calm to comfort
Sick and sorrowing.

May *the love of Jesus* fill me
As the waters fill the sea;
Him exalting, self abasing—
This is victory!

May I run the race before me,
Strong and brave to face the foe,
Looking only unto Jesus
As I onward go.

May His beauty rest upon me
As I seek the lost to win.
And may they forget the channel,
Seeing only Him.[6]

Make This Valley Full of Ditches

And yet at the same time as I yearn for this, there's another side that I want to bring to your attention. We are to reflect his loveliness—which is true and necessary—but we therefore have a specific responsibility. I had an eightieth birthday not long ago, and I received an e-mail from a friend who's about ten days older than I am. He welcomed me into what he called the Octogenarians' Club, and he wrote, "I just want you to remember one thing. There is only one rule in the Club: *retirement* is forbidden. No one retires while there's still so much work to be done." How absolutely true!

Any of you who are approaching retirement or just starting retirement or taking early retirement, are you realizing that this is the most golden opportunity in your lives? You no longer have to go to work 9 to 5 to do whatever it was you were doing. You're now free to serve Jesus full-time instead of only part-time. It's to be more, not

---

[6]Kate B. Wilkinson, "May the Mind of Christ, My Savior" (date unknown but before 1913).

less. It's to be more in his presence, more reflecting him, more telling others about Jesus. The amazing thing is that Almighty God invites us to work for him.

After I came home from Africa and it was fairly clear they were not going to quickly send me back to Africa, I was assigned a job with the mission at the home end. I asked the Lord for a verse to guide me, to give me confidence that this was his will. I was actually lying in bed in the hospital where I had just had surgery. Coming around from anesthetic, I asked the nurse, "Would you open my Bible at the place where the marker is?" She did and propped it up in front of me. I looked at the open Bible and saw that it was opened at 2 Kings 3. I thought, *How can God ever guide me from 2 Kings 3?* I started to read the chapter and was praying, "God, please, I want a verse that says, 'Thus saith the Lord.' It has to be so clear I can't miss it. It has to be so clear that when I share it with the mission they'll know it's your voice speaking." As I began to read this chapter, I realized that I knew the story—I had taught it to students in Africa. So I knew in a way what was coming, and yet I didn't know the "Thus saith the Lord" verse. Suddenly I saw it coming. "Thus saith the Lord." And I didn't want it. I was scared. I thought, *I don't know what he's going to say to me.* I put my hand across it. But then I read this amazing verse that God was speaking to the kings of Judah, Israel, and Edom through his prophet Elisha. "Thus saith the LORD, make this valley full of ditches" (v. 16, KJV).

Second Kings 3 is an amazing story. It is both exciting and beautiful. In the very next verse, after saying, "Make this valley full of ditches," God goes on to say in essence, "You're not going to see rain. You're not going to hear wind." It must have seemed awful, even stupid. There they were—an army by the dried up riverbed that separated them from the kingdom of Moab, and God was saying to soldiers who were not trained to dig ditches and who didn't even have spades, "Make this valley full of ditches." Yet as we read the story, we see that they did exactly what God told them to do. They were a well-disciplined army. So they had to get down on their knees and dig . . . with their hands. The ditches were possibly a meter long, thirty centimeters deep, ten centimeters across. I sometimes wonder, while they were all busy digging—maybe several thousand soldiers digging ditches—as each one dug his ditch, chucking the sand out, the man behind him might well have knocked the sand back in. I could just sense them getting mad with each other. Add to their discomfort the fact that God said they would not see any rain. They must have felt the whole exercise was senseless. Nevertheless, they made the valley full of ditches, and then, during the night, God filled those ditches with water. They awoke in the morning to see water throughout the valley. There was water enough for all their animals and for themselves. Meanwhile, the Moabite army on top of the hillside was looking down on the Israelite army as the early morning sun was rising. The sun shone on the water, and the Moabites saw what they thought was blood! And they said, "Incredible! The three armies down there have fought each other, and their blood fills the valley. So let's go down and take all the spoils." And they were beaten, totally devastated. God gave wonderful victory to his people.

What God said to me as I read that chapter, was, "Make this valley . . ." Now the word *this* involves the present. It's where you are now. It's not that valley of some other day in your life or that of some other person. "Make *this* valley full of ditches." If you have any sense of valley around you—it may be a new start, it may be a change of employment, there may have been sorrow, there may have been grief, there may have been all sorts of different reasons—but *this* speaks of where you are right now. It is each individual's personal valley.

Further, the word *make* is active. "Make this valley full of ditches." We have to do something, and we have to do it actively. It may well be hard work. We may well get blistered hands. We'll become thirsty, and we might get no thanks for our work. "Make this valley full of ditches."

I have been working out that verse ever since. "Make this valley full of ditches." What I have come to realize is that God doesn't actually need you and me. He is sovereign. He is almighty. He doesn't need us to reach the unreached peoples of the world. But he chooses, in his gracious mercy, to use us. He chooses to use you and me. He wants us to be *spades* in his hand. He wants us to be willing to dig his ditches, using us as his spades wherever he places us. That is amazing, quite amazing.

I belong to a youth organization in the UK, The Girl Crusaders' Union, and this organization was ninety years old last year. I was asked to take four meetings for the Union in England, Scotland, Wales, and Ireland and also one in London. The subject I was given to speak on was "God Chooses to Need Spades." We have to realize this amazing fact. He knows just *what* he wants done, he knows just *where* he wants it done, and he knows just *when* he wants it done.

Are we available? We must not get huffy if he chooses one day not to use us and takes the rake or the fork and leaves us in the tool shed. That's okay. He knows just the minute he wants us to do what he wants us to do and the niche he has for us. He wants to use all of us right through to the end.

This is to be the future for each one of us—to be 100 percent involved in serving this wonderful, lovely Lord as *his ambassadors*, taking his gospel to those whom we meet wherever we are. It is all privilege—amazing privilege. It's an unbelievable privilege that God should actually want to use you and me in his task of reaching others with the gospel.

All I have to ask is, *is my valley full yet?* Should I ever get to a moment when I say, "Dear Lord, I've been digging ditches for a long time. I'm awfully tired of it. Couldn't you give me a new verse?" he may say to me, "Your valley's not yet full." So I'm still digging ditches. Possibly what he gives you to do may seem very small. Maybe you're a housewife—just cleaning the home, cooking meals, looking after the children. You may be the breadwinner of the household—getting stuck in the traffic jams going to work in the morning, being a representative of Jesus wherever you are—in the traffic or at work. Students at college, you are to be representatives for Jesus, standing up for him, even when it's not politically correct.

So from mountaintop vision, seeking to know Christ better, to willingness to work hard down in the valleys even when our hands are blistered, empowered by his almighty resurrection power—and then to be available to him to be sent to dig ditches wherever he wants us, remembering all the time that it's a privilege to share Jesus with others in our sin-sick world—let us all "take up the whole armor of God that you may be able to withstand in the evil day, and having done all, to stand firm" (Eph. 6:13). Don't give up. Don't lose heart. Don't be discouraged. Keep on keeping on to the very end, looking unto Jesus.

I finish where I started, in Hebrews 12:1–2 (NIV).

Run with perseverance the race marked out for us [for each one of us]. Let us fix our eyes on Jesus.

And don't stop running until you hit the tape. Amen.

An Interview with Randy Alcorn, Jerry Bridges, John Piper, and Helen Roseveare

Justin Taylor

Justin Taylor: Jerry, you talked and you've written so much about the gospel being for believers for everyday life.[1] It's not just for unbelievers; it's for us in the Christian life. And you said in your talk that you didn't always believe that. At one time you thought it was just for unbelievers and it's something you begin the Christian life with. How did you make that discovery and when did it click in your mind that the gospel is also for believers?

Jerry Bridges: It really started out in the early 1960s when I was serving with The Navigators in Holland and going through some real struggles. Satan was on my back a lot, and out of sheer desperation I started preaching the gospel to myself using passages like Isaiah 53:6: "All we like sheep have gone astray. We've turned everyone to his own way. And the Lord has laid on him the iniquity of us all." I also sang some of the old gospel hymns like, "Just as I am without one plea, but that Thy blood was shed for me. O Lamb of God, I come, I come."[2] That's what I was doing, but unfortunately I did not connect the dots. I mean, I thought that it was just me. It was several years later that I realized that really what had occurred in my life was a significant paradigm shift from just thinking the gospel was for unbelievers to realizing it was for me. And then I began to share that and to teach that to other people.

Justin Taylor: When did you discover the Puritans? Could you say a little bit about what their writings have meant in your life? I'm

---

[1]See, for example, Jerry Bridges, *The Gospel for Real Life* (Colorado Springs: NavPress, 2002).
[2]Charlotte Elliot, "Just as I Am, Without One Plea" (1835).

sure many people haven't read any Puritan writings. Where would you recommend starting?

Jerry Bridges: Well, again, I discovered the Puritans in the 1960s. There was an older lady in San Diego, California, who was quite a sympathetic observer of the Navigator ministry where I was in the 1950s. And she began to send me Puritan books to read. The first one that she sent was John Owen's *Sin and Temptation*. That was such a tremendous help to me. And then she sent me Stephen Charnock's great massive volume, *The Existence and Attributes of God*. Because I was interested in the subject of holiness, I looked in the table of contents and turned immediately to the chapter on the holiness of God, a hundred pages long. When they got through with a subject, there was nothing left to be said! I started reading that chapter on the holiness of God, and I hadn't read more than a half dozen pages when I found myself down on my knees before God, just overcome with his holiness. I got up and started reading again, and a few pages later I was down on my knees again. And so that's really how I got started with them.

Justin Taylor: Whom would you recommend? If somebody wanted to start, would you recommend Charnock and Owen?

Jerry Bridges: Yes. Now, one of the beauties of Owen is that much of his work has been put in contemporary language. You yourself, Justin, have had a part in bringing *Sin and Temptation* to modern readers in its original language, but in a format that makes it more readable.[3] I think you just finished one on Owen's *Communion with God*, too.[4] I would highly recommend those books. As for Charnock, I would say you could go to the publisher Banner of Truth: any Puritan book that they've published, you can take to the bank. It's good.

Justin Taylor: Randy, I want to switch to you. Keeping on the topic of books, I know that when you travel you carry books along with you and you give them out. The Lord has used that small step of faithfulness in some really powerful ways. I wonder if you could share a story or two on that.

---

[3] John Owen, *Overcoming Sin and Temptation*, ed. Justin Taylor and Kelly Kapic (Wheaton, IL: Crossway Books, 2006).
[4] John Owen, *Communion with the Triune God*, ed. Justin Taylor and Kelly Kapic (Wheaton, IL: Crossway Books, 2007).

Randy Alcorn: For many years I have been very convinced of divine appointments, and often before I travel I'll ask the Lord, *Just put me next to the people on the plane you want me to be next to.* I meet people in airports. I meet taxi drivers. If you want to meet people from all over the world, it's taxi drivers. I have opportunities to share the gospel, and I give out books. I usually have some of my smaller books along, usually something evangelistic, sometimes different types of things.

Just last week I was in Charlotte, and there was a woman whom I shared some things with. Actually when I flew in here in Minneapolis there was a woman in the airport who had asked me a question. She was an older woman who was a little distraught because her baggage hadn't come in. I told my wife, Nanci, "You know, I feel like I should go back to that woman and bring her a book." So I took my book *50 Days of Heaven,*[5] and I walked back to her. As I was walking toward her, she was walking the other way, and she fell. I came, and several other people came, and we were able to help her out. She was put into a wheelchair, and I started talking with her, making sure she was okay. She knew I was the guy whom she had talked with earlier about the baggage. So I looked at her and I said, "You know, ma'am, the reason I came back was because I'm a writer. I just wanted to give you one of my books." I said, "Shall I put it in your bag with your baggage here?" Her husband was there with her, and she said, "Oh no. I want it now." And so she sat there and started reading it, and then she was wheeled away in the wheelchair. And I thought, *Now here's a woman who, for one thing, can actually read because she's not walking; she's being wheeled through an airport. But secondly, she just had a scary experience that reminds her of her own mortality.* And I see God do that over and over again.

One time I was walking through the airport in Chicago, and there was a girl sitting there. She was reading her Bible, and I only had one book in my briefcase. I always pray, "Lord, help me to have the right book for the right person." And it happened to be my novel *Safely Home,*[6] which I usually don't carry with me because it's a larger book. I usually carry the smaller ones. But I just felt like the Lord

---

[5]Randy Alcorn, *50 Days of Heaven* (Wheaton, IL: Tyndale House, 2006).
[6]Randy Alcorn, *Safely Home* (Wheaton, IL.: Tyndale House, 2003).

wanted me to give her this book. So I went over and said, "Hi. You don't know me. I wrote this book *Safely Home*. Here it is." I handed it to her. I was kind of late for the next connecting flight. So she said, "Well, thanks," and that was it . . . until five or six years later (about a year ago) when I got an e-mail from this gal. The e-mail came from China, and she said, "You probably don't remember me, but I was in a Chicago airport, O'Hare. You saw me reading my Bible, and you gave me a copy of your novel *Safely Home*." Well, I immediately remembered her. She went on to say, "I just wanted you to know that I read that book, and God drew me to a deeper level of commitment to Christ. He called me to study Mandarin Chinese, and I have come over as a missionary to China as a result of reading your book."

When I hear those stories, I say, "Lord, how gracious of you and how easy for me. All I did was give them a book."

I'll throw one last story in. We were on the plane on the way home from someplace. (These kind of things don't just happen on planes, but it's just the ones that are coming to mind.) There was a guy who was on his way to the University of Oregon, and he said he was Persian, of Persian descent. He was a nonbeliever. We were talking about certain things. I was having a good chat with him, and this time I had my book *Deadline*,[7] another novel I don't usually carry with me. We had a good talk about the Lord, but I didn't get into a complete gospel presentation or anything. I said, "Look, here's a novel I've written. It's got some spiritual dimensions in it. It's a murder mystery and all this kind of stuff. And you might enjoy it." And that's the last I knew of it. I prayed for him for the next few weeks or something like that, but you know, people drop off your prayer list. You lose touch with them and all that. Well, I was speaking a couple of years ago at my home church in Oregon. This gal comes up to me and says, "Are you Randy?" I said yes. She said, "Well, I'm going to tell you a story. I know you don't know this because this guy told me he's never told you or tried to contact you. But do you remember a guy, a Persian guy, and you gave him your novel?" "Oh sure," I said. "Yeah, I remember him." And she said, "Well, he got down to the University of Oregon. It turns out he was one night early. He went to his room. Nobody was there. Nobody was there in the whole dorm.

---

[7]Randy Alcorn, *Deadline* (Sisters, OR: Multnomah, 1999).

And he was totally by himself, totally bored. So he takes your book. He reads through your book through the night. In the middle of the night when a character in the book, Jake Woods, is reading *Mere Christianity* and bows his knees, confesses his sins, and gives his life to Christ, this guy did the same thing: he got down on his knees, confessed his sins, and gave his life to Christ." I'm hearing this, and I'm thinking, *Wow*. But then she says this: "And I want you to know that that young man is the godliest man I have ever met." So in other words, it wasn't just a conversion story; it turned out that the fruit of the Spirit has been born in his life. I haven't met the guy. Maybe I won't meet him again, until heaven.

God is so gracious to do these things. I think we're not going to hear most of these kinds of stories until we're in heaven with him. And what a great thing that will be.

Justin Taylor: Dr. Roseveare, is there a particular missionary biography that has impacted your life or a missionary biography that you would particularly recommend for people?

Helen Roseveare: Isabel Kuhn. I can't remember the title any longer, but it was marvelous. Any of her books. I'm from a slightly older generation than most of you, though I go back to Hudson Taylor (if possible the original Hudson Taylor double volume). Also Amy Carmichael, and anything that's come from Dohnavur.

Justin Taylor: Let me ask you about being single and about women who are single. I know there are a number of women who struggle in their singleness. Could you give any counsel on remaining faithful through the long journey in singleness, and how those two relate?

Helen Roseveare: Those of you who are single and want me to say something else, you won't like what I'm going to say: *It is a privilege*. God has been so good to me. Okay, there have been one or two occasions where it would have been rather nice if I had a husband. Not that I really wanted a husband; I wanted a man about the house to mend a chair leg when it broke! But quite honestly, the Lord Jesus has been my all-sufficiency all through. And it is a privilege, because as single on the mission field, I was able to do things that I certainly would not have been able to do had I been married, had a family, and had responsibilities for a home. I was free. I could go into any African home. I didn't have to look first or think, *Is there a leprosy* *patient here who might take infection to my family?* I could just go in. I didn't have to look at my watch to see that I got home on time to make the kids' evening meal. I was free, and God blessed that so richly. He gave me African sisters who've been closer to me than any blood sister ever was. I've had friendships with them on a level that I'm sure I wouldn't have had in the same way had I been married. It's been a privilege.

Just keep your eyes on Jesus. And never allow anybody to suggest to you or say to you or even think about you that God gives you second best. God doesn't know the phrase "second best." He's promised you *his* best.

Justin Taylor: We've talked in the conference so far about our own deaths and enduring until the end. But I know that the death of people we love is a major challenge for our own faithfulness. And I think of people who say, "If I lost a child, if I lost a spouse, if my mother died, I don't know how I could go on." How do you counsel people in those situations? John and Jerry, I know you've each experienced situations of death, of people you love very dearly. So how have you worked through that and remained faithful? And how do you counsel people in that sort of grief that challenges their faithfulness?

Jerry Bridges: I'm more of a teacher than a pastor, of course. In fact, I'm not a pastor at all. I have not ever been, so I don't find myself in those situations very often. But I go back to what I said in my talk. We have to cling to the promises of God that he said he will never leave us or forsake us (Heb. 13:5) and nothing can separate us from his love (Rom. 8:35–39). That, along with 2 Corinthians 12:9: "My grace is sufficient for you, for my power is made perfect in weakness." This year I'm actually walking along with a friend of mine whose wife died January 1, and those are the passages I keep bringing up to him, along with the fact that God does all things well.

John Piper: I wasn't sure whether you were asking one or two questions, so let me take them both. How do you counsel a person who says, "I don't know what I would do if my child died"? That's one person. And the other one, their child already did die. In the first person's case, you have some time before it happens, and what you want to do as a pastor is build into their lives the kind of vision of God and his sovereignty and his goodness that gets them ready. I consider that one of my main responsibilities at Bethlehem: to so preach and so teach and so live as to prepare people to suffer. And suffering, the hardest kind, is losing what's precious to you, whether it's your own health or somebody else's life. I think that if someone says something like that, that's a signal for those who have any input into their life. It may be off the cuff, but it's usually a signal that, biblically, they don't have all the pieces in place yet to settle their soul to say, "I do know what I would do. I would throw myself on God. That's what I would do. Weeping my eyes out, I would throw myself on God, and he'd be enough." That's what they would say. That's what I would do.

If it's already happened, then you've got the question, where are they theologically and spiritually? Are they angry at God? Are they despairing? Or are they a rock? Try to discern that as to the timing and the nature of your comments. But mainly, get your arms around people and hold them until enough time goes by that there's enough . . . I don't know what to call it. I don't want to say "healing" or "steadying." But time is amazing in what it does to the horror of a moment. Time. An hour makes a difference. A day makes a difference. A week makes a difference, and a month makes a difference, and ten years make a difference.

I spoke with one man down here who knew that we did the funeral this past Wednesday for my stillborn granddaughter. And he said, "Tomorrow is the twenty-first birthday of our stillborn son." Think of that. For twenty-one years they've not known this baby, and they still mark the day because that's how long the pain can last. And yet, as he signified, it's a totally different experience today than it was then. Time has an amazing effect on that.

What you want to do with anybody is hold them up while that time passes. Hold them up. They may want to just run out in front of a car or throw themselves off a cliff, but you're going to grab them and you're not going to let that happen. Tell them, "I've got you. I'm for you. I'm your strength right now on behalf of Jesus." Hold them long enough, and don't necessarily say anything. Then discern what they need you to say. As a pastor, I have no canned speeches. Zero. I have no filing system: "Death of baby talk"; "death of wife talk." I don't have any files like that.

So when a man in our church lost his wife of about thirty-six years, about five weeks into it I thought, *Perhaps today he needs a word.* And I wrote a fairly long letter, about three-fourths of a single-spaced page, and sent it to him. He called me up, and we went out to lunch. He just poured out his heart about how significant that letter was. You know, most of the comfort ends after about two, three, or four weeks, and then you have to navigate life, and life feels totally different. Nobody knows quite what to say to you, and so the fact that anybody would stop and try to say anything by way of empathy five weeks later is really significant.

Justin Taylor: Dr. Roseveare, a lot of people think about missions and feel called to missions but fear the prospect of suffering. They might read the biographies that you mentioned or read your own works and have a genuine fear of suffering. They know that they're doing the Christian life here in America, doing okay and remaining faithful, and they're wondering, *If I go overseas and I undergo tremendous suffering, I don't know what will happen, and I fear that.* How would you speak to somebody who's wavering between staying here and going to another country?

Helen Roseveare: I know that the evening that I came to know the Lord Jesus as my Savior, seven o'clock in the evening, I was at a youth house party over the Christmas holidays from college. I went downstairs at the evening meeting, and somebody said, "What's happened to you?" I guess I was just so overwhelmed at the wonder that God loved me so much he sent Jesus to die for me. I was given a Bible, and it was the first Bible I ever owned. The man who'd been doing the Bible studies at the house party, Dr. Graham Scroggie, wrote in the flyleaf of my Bible, *Philippians 3:10.* For some of you today I've been signing books, and you'll find *Philippians 3:10* is written in because that was my verse that was given to me. First he quoted the verse to me: "That I may know him, and the power of his resurrection, and the fellowship of his sufferings, being made conformable unto his death." And then he said, "Tonight you started that verse, 'that I may know Christ.' My prayer for you in the years that lie ahead is that you'll know more and more of the power of his resurrection." He was a very straight, upright man, and then very quietly, looking straight at me, he said, "Maybe one day God will give you the privilege to know something of the fellowship of his sufferings." I'd been a Christian half an hour and I was told that it was a privilege to suffer for Jesus.

Ever since then, I think that the word *privilege* has stayed with me possibly more than any one word in my Christian life. It's a *privilege*. It's a privilege that he saved me. It's a privilege that he's allowed me to have any part in talking to others about him. Everything has been privilege, and I was told the same night that I came to know Jesus as my Savior that it's a privilege to have fellowship in his sufferings. I fear that in today's climate we—that's any of us who have the privilege of speaking to others, encouraging others to accept Jesus as their Savior—we don't underline straightaway that the Christian life will involve suffering. In our country we don't really know what persecution is, but in Muslim countries we expect new Christians to accept suffering, and we think it's very marvelous of them. We don't think about it for ourselves, but we should all of us know that if we love the Lord Jesus, he himself said, "If you're going to follow me, take up your cross and follow me." And where was he going? He was going to Calvary. And we follow him there.

The death-to-the-self life—the death to our ambition and our rights to be who or what or where we wish; the giving of that over to Jesus and letting him really live his life in and through us under any circumstance—will involve suffering. I believe the Savior suffers today for the millions of unreached, untouched people who have never yet even heard his name. And he invites us. It's such a privilege. It's such a privilege to be invited to share with him in his sufferings.

I've got no panacea to offer you. I've got no way of saying you won't suffer. You will suffer. You should suffer if you're really a Christian. Christians are indwelt by Jesus, and he suffers.

Justin Taylor: Randy, what are some practical strategies you use in your own life, or have used or encourage others to use, for cultivating courage? For people who fear man, who want to avoid suffering or are in love with comfort, what are some practical things we can do to be more courageous?

Randy Alcorn: I think one thing is when God lays something on your heart. It kind of relates to something I said earlier about the instruments or members of your body. For instance, you're in a situation. Many of us are in these situations where we're around somebody—maybe it's at a bus stop, maybe we're at a restaurant, or maybe we meet somebody somewhere—whatever it is, we feel this inclination from the Lord, *You know, I should say something about Jesus. I should share my faith or at least get the ball rolling here with something.* What I tell people and what I experience in my own life is that you need to open your mouth and start talking. The big battle is what precedes that, not what follows that. Because once you've committed yourself that you're going to be talking about Jesus, now you can talk about Jesus. But what holds us back? *O Lord, help me to, oh, to, you know . . . could I just . . . ?* But once you get it going, then it goes somewhere. With courage, it's often that you just simply need to take the step.

My wife is very courageous. She's very courageous because she does not like to fly on airplanes, and many people who don't like to fly on airplanes just don't. But she does. It takes no courage for me to fly on an airplane because I don't fear it. What takes courage is when you fear something and then do it anyway. And that's exactly what I think we so often lack in the Christian life. We ask ourselves, "Should we speak up?" I tell college kids who are in college classrooms that it's not healthy for them to be in their classrooms and hear professors day after day defame the name of Christ and not speak up. You must speak up and confess Christ before men. If you do, you will experience growth and reward. You'll have other kids in the class say, "Yeah, I feel that way, too." They'll start speaking up, too.

God rewards courage, but it's that first step. Tell God, "I'm just going to do it, and now I'm going to trust you to help me. I'm not going to wait until you miraculously open my mouth. I have to do it and go forward."

Justin Taylor: Jerry, you've spent decades now working with college students. I'm sure you've seen many changes over the years. What encourages you the most and what concerns you the most about the current generation?

Jerry Bridges: I would say what encourages me most is that, on the one hand, I believe there is a genuine hunger, particularly among Christian young people who have come to know Christ. They do want to grow, and they do want to be involved. In our own organization, The Navigators, we have hundreds of students every summer who are going on short-term mission trips and things like this.

Contrary to that, I think the thing that is most concerning is the students, both outside and inside the church, who simply have no notion of sin. They just go along with the world, and as long as it's not really flagrant or outside of the box, so to speak, of the culture in which they're living, anything goes. There's no shame regarding immorality and things like that, and that's very distressing. I was asked to speak to a student group in a particular state, and the campus minister said to me privately, "I'm really concerned that immorality has begun to penetrate within our group here." And that of course is a tremendous concern today. Obviously, in our culture what the Bible calls immorality is just assumed to be commonplace. There's absolutely no shame attached to it. And the students are falling in line with this.

Justin Taylor: Can you tell us a little bit about your book *Respectable Sins*[8] and what motivated you to write that?

Jerry Bridges: The respectable sins are sins that Christians tolerate in their lives—pride, a critical spirit, a judgmental spirit, selfishness, gossip, impatience, anger, an unforgiving spirit—these kinds of things. The reason I wrote that book is because as I look at the broad stream of the Christian community, it seems to me that we have begun to define sin in terms of the flagrant sins that are being committed out there in society. We do not see our own sins. This is not to lessen the seriousness of those flagrant sins by any means, but we can get upset about, for example, a major denomination that ordains a practicing homosexual as a bishop, but we don't get upset about our gossip and our pride and our critical spirit. And that's what motivated me to write the book.

Justin Taylor: John, this final question is for you. I know in an audience this size there are people who have come here maybe as an act of desperation, ready to throw in the towel on their marriage or the ministry they're involved with, or throw in the towel on Christ himself. If you could speak to that person or those people, how would you counsel them at this time?

John Piper: Well, it's not God's will that you throw in the towel on your marriage. It might be God's will that it might be time for a

---

[8]Jerry Bridges, *Respectable Sins* (Colorado Springs: NavPress, 2007).

change in your ministry, but if you're thinking in terms of towel toss-
ing, it's probably not time. So that's the first thing I'd say: *Don't do
it yet.*

Then I think I would say to ask God against all human expecta-
tion, though your marriage may seem hopeless and the ministry may
seem hopeless, to give you grace to persevere. Pray, "Keep me. Keep
me. Do a miracle. I don't know how you would do it. I don't know
what it would feel like, but do a miracle." I have seen in relationships
with children, spouses, and churches that you can come to a point
where the whole emotional framework of the relationship looks to
all rational appearances as though there is no way forward. At that
moment Satan will say, *That's exactly right. There is no way forward.*
And you have to have a view of God that says he "calls into existence
the things that do not exist" (Rom. 4:17). There are some situations
where there is no human solution. Jesus said, "With man it is impossible" (Mark 10:27). So if I'm looking at a couple in my office and
they say it's impossible, I say, "You're right." So we'll just start there.
But we're believers in the living God, we believe in supernatural reality. God brought the universe out of nothing, and he can bring hope
in a marriage out of nothing. You do not feel that as a rational or
emotional possibility at this moment. But because God is God, I'm
asking you to simply to ask him to do that.

Then go to his Word and look for evidences of his patience, evidences of his grace, verses like that. That's where I would go. God's
God-ness creates a future where there is none. Out of nothing, he
brings something. Nothing you could tell me—no eighteen prosti-
tutes in your spouse's experience, or serial adulteries, or "he turned
out to be gay"—nothing you could tell me would make me say this
is impossible. I will never say that about a covenant-keeping relationship, because we are called to model Christ and the church. Christ
will never divorce his church. She may abandon him, but he will never
divorce his church. He has the power to bring her back. You don't
have that power, but God has the power to bring out of nothing that
which is both in church situations and marital situations.

I know a situation right now very close to this conference where
the teenage boy believes he's gay and is wanting to die. That's all he
wants. He doesn't want anything else. His parents are absolutely

desperate. They don't know if they'll find him dead at any given day. And I spoke into that parent's heart: *There's hope here. This boy is gay or not gay. Maybe he is wired to delight in men. All right. I'm wired to be really feisty with my wife. There is a future in this battle. He needs to feel hope. He can feel hope. God can bring something out of nothing.* Some situations feel absolutely hopeless and we feel absolutely powerless. But if Christianity has to go with that kind of flow, we're just packing up our bags. We're quitting. If God can't bring to bear on this world a supernatural reality that breaks through those situations, then what do we have to offer? We're just a bunch of secular psychological massagers of people's needs and have relative degrees of making their lives better, but as far as eternal reality, God will break in.

Finally, find someone. Go down to the prayer room. Share as much of your situation as you can. Get two or three people around you, hands on your shoulders, and ask God for a miracle.

Justin Taylor: Would you please close in prayer?

John Piper: Father, right now those kinds of situations abound, and so I want to get my hand out there right now on every shoulder where it feels hopeless. And I ask that you would come with an awakening, a mustard seed of hope. *All right. God is God. I see no way forward. Make a door in the sky. Spread a banquet in the wilderness. Make quail come out of nowhere. May waters of the sea divide. May the sun stop in its course. May these five loves feed five thousand.* So, Lord, do an amazing work. We don't want to just talk about endurance. We want to see your mighty hand bring people through this present crisis out into a day of embattled hope. We pray this in Jesus' name. Amen.

An Interview with
John Piper and John MacArthur

Justin Taylor

Justin Taylor: Dr. MacArthur and Dr. Piper, do you remember when you met each other for the first time or when you became aware of each other's ministries?

John Piper: I think I remember. He wouldn't remember. There he was screaming away years and years ago, and I didn't like him. He was just too harsh for me. He came to speak at Bethel College in the late seventies, and we had breakfast together with John Sailhamer. That's the first time we ever met. Since I saw him as an expositor instead of an evangelist, I asked him the question, "If you were starting over, how would you make sure evangelism happened in your local church?" And I think his answer was, "The first staff member I would add would be an evangelist." That's my memory of our first encounter at a restaurant somewhere up in New Brighton, Minnesota.

John MacArthur: He's right: I don't remember that! I hate to say that. But there was a real highlight in my life, and he was a part of that highlight. When I wrote *The Gospel According to Jesus*, I was so exercised because that "no lordship" theology was coming out of the heritage that was my heritage in a sense. When I wrote that book I didn't know anybody outside of my circles really, and I didn't know how this book would be received. But Jim Boice agreed to write the foreword, and John Piper wrote an endorsement that was absolutely stunning to me, because I was really not moving in Reformed circles at that time. I was a leaky dispensationalist. That was my world, and I realized that I was much more one of you than I was one of them. So I was so overwhelmed that John gave such a good, encouraging endorsement to that. And, of course, from then on I have read and followed his ministry with joy and gratitude.

Another one of the little highlights in my life was when we had a little meeting down in Louisville, and John got the assignment to pray for me. I was so blessed just to have him pray for me. I'll never forget that.

Justin Taylor: I was looking this morning at the dates for both of your fathers: Dr. Jack MacArthur, 1914–2005; Dr. Bill Piper, 1919–2007—almost the exact same lifespan. They both had honorary doctorates from Bob Jones. They were both Baptists, and both traveling evangelists. Tell us about their examples, the lessons that you both remember from your dads on faithfulness and endurance, or particular things that stick out to you that have impacted your ministry and life.

John Piper: When you say that, I would just love to have heard John MacArthur's dad. I don't think I ever did.

I could talk forever about my dad. The main distinctive about my dad's evangelism is that it was so doctrinal. He was Bible-saturated in the dispensational school, but very doctrinal, which is why he was different. He did his evangelism by developing the doctrine of regeneration, or the doctrine of hell, or the doctrine of heaven, or the doctrine of repentance. That's the way he thought. And so I grew up assuming that's the way you handle the Bible. That's what you do. Even if you do evangelism, if you shepherd a church, you take the Bible and you find what it means across its terrain and its coherency, and that's what reality is. It was an awesome privilege to grow up in a home where my dad would leave for two, three weeks. He crossed the country in those days for five or six weeks, came home for four days, eight days, and then left again. A lot of people get bent out of shape at their dad's this or that, but I never, ever resented my father's ministry, though he was only home a third of the time. It seemed like an awesome privilege to me.

I think the key there was that my mom loved his ministry. She never bad-mouthed him. She never said, "Where is he? He never comes home." Never was there any of that. Growing up, I just assumed that my dad had a call on his life, and that was it. My job with my mom was to back him up. When he came home he told the stories of the victories of the gospel. And what could be better? He also brought jokes with him. We'd sit at the table, and he'd give me his latest joke.

John MacArthur: I think the thing that always stood out in my mind was, just on a personal side, how much my dad loved my mother. It was just a treasure to me. I learned how you're supposed to love your wife. He just loved her, and he loved his children in a unique way—very endearing qualities. He was an evangelist with Fuller Foundation, with the Charles E. Fuller traveling evangelists around the States. He was also an evangelist at Moody in the years when William Culbertson was president there. He traveled all over, doing city-wide meetings all over the Midwest and East. He graduated from Eastern Seminary in Philadelphia, so he had all kinds of Eastern connections.

I had the same kind of experience as a kid living in California with my dad going away for long periods of time on the train and doing city-wide meetings and gatherings here and there. He even went overseas a couple of times to do some meetings. And like you, John, I never resented that. It was just a wonderful thing when he left, and a wonderful thing when he came home.

But eventually he became a pastor, and I had the privilege to sit under his ministry from my junior high years on. He was an expositor through Matthew, through Romans, through John, and always with an apologetic bent. He was always leaning hard on evidences for biblical veracity, always trying to answer the critic, the person who had reasons not to believe the Bible. Everything was laced with that, and that became the predominant emphasis of his radio ministry in the last years. He was on the radio program *Voice of Calvary* for sixty-some years. He was faithful. He used to start the program by playing the marimba. He played the theme at the beginning and the end and preached in the middle.

Justin Taylor: Did your fathers both want or expect you to be pastors? If so, did they ever express that desire to you?

John MacArthur: My father never put pressure on me to be a pastor. He loved the ministry. He loved the church. He loved the people in the church. He loved to preach. He loved to read and study. He was a voracious reader, and he just loved his ministry. So I grew up with a man who loved everything he did, and yet he never put any pressure on me because he always felt that only the Lord could do that, and he didn't want to cloud my thinking. Because I think I had such great respect for him, I think he backed far away from that.

But the time came in my life through a car accident. When I was eighteen I got thrown out of a car and went about 120 yards down the middle of a highway and survived. I spent three months in bed. That was a time when the Lord really got hold of my heart. My dad never put pressure on me, but once I committed to that, I became his personal project. And then he got serious.

Justin Taylor: Do you remember the conversation you had when you told him you felt called to gospel ministry?

John MacArthur: I don't remember the exact conversation, but somewhere around there he gave me a Bible, and he just wrote in it, "Dear Johnny, Preach the Word. Love, Dad." That was the one thing he wanted to say to me: *Preach the Word*. And we had that conversation about 2 Timothy 4, about preaching the Word all the way to the end and being faithful to the end. That's how his father had been, and that's the goal that he wanted for his own life.

I was basically a football jock in my high school days and even in college, and then my dad dragged me off to seminary. He said, "You have to go to seminary. You have to get serious and go to seminary, and you need to go to Talbot Seminary because there's this guy there named Charles Feinberg." Do you remember the name? He was brilliant. He studied fourteen years to be a rabbi and then was converted to Christ. Feinberg earned two doctorates. He went to Dallas Seminary and got his ThD, and then he left there and went to Johns Hopkins. He studied for his PhD under William Foxwell Albright, who is a great Middle Eastern archaeologist. And so my dad had worked a deal with Feinberg to take me on as a personal project while I was in seminary.

Feinberg called me into his office periodically in honor of my dad. He didn't tell me he was doing it because of my dad, but I know my dad was behind the scenes, trying to shift my mental focus. Feinberg would give me books to read, and he would have conversations with me, and I was even in his home. I became a good friend of his son Paul, and also with his son John. We spent a lot of time together. I had to preach my first year in seminary in chapel before the whole student body, and Feinberg chose the text. He gave me 2 Samuel 7, the great Davidic promise. So I preached on "presuming on God." You know, "Nathan said, 'Go build it,' and God said, 'Nathan, I don't want him to do it; he's a man of blood,'" and so forth. I preached on presuming on God—and I completely missed the point! The point was the Davidic covenant, not presuming on God. That was trivial.

When I finished, Feinberg gave me a sheet, and he wrote in red, "You missed the entire point of the passage. See me in my office." I went into the office, and I'm telling you, he shredded me as only he could. And you know, that was the greatest lesson I ever learned. He said, "To get the point of the passage is all we're asking out of you. That's *all* we're asking. We don't want your creativity; just get the point of the passage."

When Feinberg went to be with the Lord some years ago, his family called and asked if I would speak at the funeral. So I guess somewhere along the line he told somebody that he thought I was getting the point of the passage. They felt free to ask me to speak!

Justin Taylor: Dr. Piper, can you tell us about the time when you wrote a letter to your father telling him about your decision to go into pastoral ministry?

John Piper: Never in my memory did my dad urge me to be a pastor. In fact, when I chose to leave teaching in 1979 and head to the pastorate, he wrote a page-and-a-half letter to dissuade me, because after being in a thousand churches, he was afraid for me. He just said, "You have found your niche. I wanted to name you Peter, but your mother wouldn't let me name you Peter Piper. We named you John, and that's who you are. You're the quiet, reflective type. You're not the proclaimer. And so you belong in the classroom. Stay there, because you're going to be eaten alive in the church." That was the letter. But I couldn't resist the call, and when I said, "Daddy, I think I'm going to do this anyway," he said, "Good. I just want to make sure!" That was the approach that he took.

He took that exact same approach when we were about to adopt a little girl when I was fifty years old. I said, "I'm going to adopt a little girl." He wrote me a two-and-a-half page letter discouraging me from adoption. He thought I was too old and that the next phase of life would be more fruitful if I was an empty-nester. I thought seriously about what he wrote and called him on the phone to get it mouth to mouth. But in the end we were deeply persuaded this was God's call on our life. The first time my father met Talitha, before she was a year old, she leaned into his arms and won him over completely. He never said another word, and loved her like his other grandchildren.

So my dad, I guess, has a different way of encouraging in ministry. He really thought I had found my niche in teaching, and I think he was wrong about that.

Justin Taylor: If you could go back now to when you started pastoral ministry and talk to the thirty-four-year-old John Piper and the twenty-nine-year-old John MacArthur, knowing what you know now, what do you think would be the most important thing to tell them on the front end of their ministries?

John Piper: It's clear to me that the most important things would have to do with my children and my wife, and not the church. I don't think I would do anything basically differently at Bethlehem. If I thought real hard about it, I might think of some tactical changes. But I think we work out of a pastoral model that's so simple, it's hard to change it. You open the Bible, and you tell people what it means with all your heart, and you try to live it out before the people and figure out the other stuff as you go along.

But I could do better on my family. I could really do better as a dad, I think, if I started over again. Nobody was talking in terms of "shepherding a child's heart" in those days.[1] Here's an illustration: Rick Gamache is a pastor of a Sovereign Grace church here in Minneapolis. Rick taught my class for me last Thursday and told these guys about questions that he asks his children to draw out their heart.[2] I read those ten questions or so, and I copied them down and

---

[1] See Ted Tripp, *Shepherding a Child's Heart* (Wapwallopen, PA: Shepherd Press, 1995).
[2] Here are the questions provided by Pastor Gamache:

How are your devotions?
What is God teaching you?
In your own words, what is the gospel?
Is there a specific sin you're aware of that you need my help defeating?
Are you more aware of my encouragement or my criticism?
What's Daddy most passionate about?
Do I act the same at church as I do when I'm at home?
Are you aware of my love for you?
Is there any way I've sinned against you that I've not repented of?
Do you have any observations for me?
How am I doing as a dad?
How have Sunday's sermons impacted you?
Does my relationship with Mom make you excited to be married?

(Gamache writes, "On top of these things, with my older kids, I'm always inquiring about their relationships with their friends and making sure God and his gospel are the center of those relationships. And I look for every opportunity to praise their mother and increase their appreciation and love for her.")

sent them to all four of my sons. They all have kids, and I don't want them to do as poorly as I did. I think I was faithful to my kids. I went to all the soccer games. I tucked them in at night. I set an example for them. I had devotions every night. But I rarely drew out their affectional life at age thirteen, fourteen, or fifteen. And that has not set them up to be as effective in their lives as they might have been, I think.

So I would go to the John Piper at age thirty-four, and I would say, "Do better at supplementing your truth commitments with drawing out your wife's heart and drawing out your child's heart, so that they find ways to express what's in the heart, not just what's in the mind." I think I was naive about that because all that stuff sort of comes naturally for me. I'm an emotional guy. It's easy for me to express emotions—positive, negative, I'm all over the map. But it doesn't come naturally for everyone. You have to draw it out. So that's the first thing that comes to my mind because it feels big now, and the boys are all grown. I still have my daughter Talitha, which is a wonderful gift. That's why I copied these ten questions down, because she's eleven and it's not too late.

John MacArthur: I think there's some of that with me. There was a lot less introspection spiritually going on in evangelicalism when I was twenty-nine and coming into my church. I don't think people thought much about expressing feelings, at least in the world that I lived in. So I would think that would probably be more true of me too than it would be in later years.

I'm not a high-powered, Type A, steamroller guy, but I'm highly motivated—I don't know whether it's a natural gift or a spiritual gift—to organize everything. I think now I've let all of that go, and now I see that there's a simple, natural flow to the life of the church, but in the early years I was always trying to reorganize everything and restructure it, moving people around in different boxes. I finally figured out that that's not what you should be doing, but I think the price was paid to some degree with my family because I was so busy studying, and then on top I was coming up with all these different ways to structure and organize things. I don't think I gave the time to my wife Patricia in particular; even though I was home, I was preoccupied. I was trying to stuff so many things in. The joke in our family is "Calling Father." They'd wave their fingers across my face . . . even when I was there. I wasn't always easy to engage, although I think I'm better at it now. You'd have to ask them. I hope I am.

I think from the church's standpoint, patience was a challenge for me. I've never been a really patient person with myself, particularly when I was young and expected everything to happen fast; I was disappointed if it didn't happen at the pace that I thought it should happen. Why can't people figure it out? Here it is; do it. Our church is Grace Community Church, but I was struggling with *grace*. Hopefully I've come to understand that a little better, and I now have more patience with people. I was mentioning this to somebody earlier: Pastors must preach the Word in a way that is strong and hard and bold and clear and straightforward and without compromise, and then apply it with tenderness and compassion and grace and long-suffering with people. In the pulpit, it's clear; it's hard-hitting; it's firm. But when you come down and you shepherd these people, that's where, in the application of these great truths, you have to express the patience that endears them. You love them in the process and move them along gradually. And that's something I had to learn.

Justin Taylor: You both receive a tremendous amount of praise— and a tremendous amount of criticism. How do you personally handle both the reception of praise and the reception of criticism? How do you keep from being prideful on the one hand, and overly discouraged on the other hand? How do you process that when a high praise comes in or a harsh criticism so that you're responding biblically?

John MacArthur: This whole thing is a mercy. My salvation is a mercy. I'm not worthy of any of this. And I'm always amazed that God does what he does. Who's adequate for these things? I think you just have to deal with things honestly and realistically, in the sense that God is not doing work on the basis of my abilities and my gifts and my power and my insight. I'm just a tool or an instrument.

I think part of the benefit of being in the same church for a long time is it reflects back all your strengths and weaknesses. If you just go from town to town to town, you might believe your press clippings, but if you have to live continuously with the failures, with the inadequacies, with the weaknesses in your own life that show up reflected in your people and your family and your kids, I think there's something real about that. It helps to have a wife who knows that praise can be harmful, and without seeking to be a thorn in the flesh, she can also be the one who pulls you back to reality.

When people say kind things about me, I know that they're responding to the teaching of the Word of God and the work of the Spirit through the Word. And I'm just grateful. It always surprises me, and I'm grateful.

On the other hand, I decided a long time ago not to try to defend myself against criticism. If the truth were known, I can't defend myself at some points. I don't want to get in a situation where I'm trying to portray some kind of perfection or answer every critic. We all have weaknesses. I have errors in my theology. I don't know where they are. If I knew where they were, I would change them! I don't know where they are, but I'm working on it. Twenty-five years ago I resolved to refuse to defend myself. I just try to do what I do and be faithful and let my life and ministry speak for itself instead of running around trying to answer every accusation and criticism that comes. I understand that they're out there. I don't look for them. If they come, I'll sometimes write a letter that will say, "Thank you for causing me to examine my own heart. I appreciate what you said, and I want you to know that I took it seriously. Thank you." That's about it. You need to embrace those kinds of things because those things keep you humble.

John Piper: I would just make sure we hear both sides of the word *mercy*. If praise comes, the doctrine of God's sovereign mercy means that you must channel all the praise to him, because without him nothing would be happening of any eternal significance. Sovereign mercy pulls the plug on the compliment terminating with me.

It also works for criticism, because what's devastating about criticism is that it seems to undo your standing with God or usefulness in the ministry. And since God gives us ministry by mercy and saves us by mercy, therefore, criticism can't do that. It can't. People can't pull the plug on that because I can roll not only the burdens of my pressures onto the Lord but also the burdens of my sin. I find it very helpful in counseling—and I counsel myself every day—that when somebody is feeling guilt for, say, the suicide of their son or a divorce or whatever, and they ask me, "Should I be feeling guilty?" I tell them

that I don't know, and it doesn't matter. If you spend your time trying to figure out whether you should be feeling guilty, you'll always
come up with an ambiguity. Just relax and feel guilty, and then deal
with it the only way that you'll be able to deal with it at the judgment
day, because I promise you at the judgment day you'll feel guilty.
Everything will be exposed. The heart will be laid bare. You'll have no
argument at all. Guilty. And if you don't have a solution for that issue
now, you may not then. So let's just relax. We're guilty as charged.
And now I repent. That's a little bit of an oversimplification, because
we're not guilty of some things that we're accused of. Therefore, we
have to have people around us.

I'm surrounded by people who, I pray, are not "yes men" at
Bethlehem. I have a staff. They hear what I hear, and they can say,
"Yeah, you probably should take that into account. That has some
validity to it." Or they say, "Blow that away. We don't see it that
way." So having a community really, really matters.

Finally, there is a theological paradox that people don't like to
hear. But I think the Lord works on my pride by letting me sin so
much. There are so many words that come out of my mouth toward
my wife, so many feelings I have toward people, that when I go on
my face and I do this conscience thing, I don't know how I could say
what Paul said: "I have served to this day with a clear conscience"
(2 Tim. 1:3). What planet does this guy live on? Is he in touch? I mean,
there are women in the world. Ever had a thought? Good night! I
think he must mean something like, "I keep real short accounts."
I mean, a totally clear conscience, Paul? Give me a break. Am I being
blasphemous here toward the Word of God?

John MacArthur: I think he dealt with it. In Romans 7 he said, "I
do what I don't want to do and I don't do what I ought to do, and
I'm a wretched man."

John Piper: And he had a guilty conscience.

John MacArthur: Yeah. But he dealt with his sin. It didn't accu-
mulate.

John Piper: And that's the point I took away: a cultivated, secret
life of sin is the killer. (Not that you never have a thought that you're
ashamed of or that you never say a word that you're ashamed of.) So
anyway, my point was that as I go on my face morning after morn-

ing, I have so much stuff to deal with here that I can't be pointing my finger too many places. And so when I stand in line down here and people say, "Thank you, thank you, thank you, thank you," I know what's going on at home. I know what's going on in my heart. I have so much stuff to deal with. I'm just saying, "Amazing. Amazing." Like you said, John: if anybody gets saved, you just want to stand back and feel the thunder.

Justin Taylor: So many young pastors and missionaries look up to both of you and read your books. As you counsel young men and women on the mission field, it seems like one of the truisms is that circumstances often confirm our calling. And if you're good at something, fruit often comes with that. You've both had incredibly fruitful ministries. How do you think through the issues of faithfulness and fruitlessness? Take someone out there is who is in a small church, or on the mission field, and a year goes by, two years go by with no converts, no apparent fruit. How should they think through the possibility that this might not be their gifting, they need to pull back from that, there's no fruit being produced, versus the perspective that they need to stick it out for another ten years, twenty years, thirty years?

John MacArthur: Well, there are several ways to answer that question. But first of all, I'm not in charge of the results. Paul says, "If our gospel be hid, it's hid to the eyes of those that have been blinded by Satan" (cf. 2 Cor. 4:4). I can't overpower that. I learned this concept as a football player. I wanted to win the game. I always wanted to win the game. That was the whole point of playing. You don't play to lose; you play to win. That was a given. But I couldn't guarantee the win, because there were eleven people on the other side of the ball trying to stop me from doing what I wanted to do and ten people on my own team who sometimes didn't do the right thing either. It was way beyond my capability to achieve the end. So at some point I determined that all I could control was effort. I could not control outcome.

Early in my first year or so at Grace Community Church, I had this little kind of motto that I used: "If you concentrate on the *depth* of your ministry, God will take care of the *breadth* of it." My ministry hasn't changed since that first year in that small, little church. For me, it's all about getting into the depth of Scripture and my own personal walk with the Lord. Breadth is something that God does, and I think you've got to come to that, or you're going to frustrate yourself when you compare yourself with all kinds of other people and other situations. That's not to say that if nothing happens God wants you to stay there. He may want you to move. But that becomes a personal decision to be made with much prayer and perhaps some counsel.

I think we have to be content with *effort* and leave *outcome* to the Lord. That's where you're going to find your contentment. It's like anything else. If you're only content with numbers, then no number will bring you contentment, because there will always be somebody who has more, somebody who's more popular, somebody who's more well known. You've got to focus on the issue of faithfulness in the effort to which you've been called. Again, we need to get back to the idea of mercy and just realize that God rewards faithfulness.

John Piper: I think of the stories we hear about people like Robert Morrison. He was the first Protestant missionary to China. And this is the two hundredth anniversary of Protestant missionaries to China. He waited seven years before his first convert. Same with Adoniram Judson: he also waited seven years before his first convert. David Brainerd experienced the same thing. There are a handful of these guys, and their stories are told over and over again. What's forgotten is that you don't choose to go to the mission field wondering if you will have gifts. Gifts are verified at home before you go. So I presume that the church, the community of believers in which these men were saved and began to mature, spotted spiritual gifts in them. I think that the function of the church in the discovery of our gifts and calling is to *confirm gifts.* And what's confirmed is not a skill that is ineffective. That's not a spiritual gift, I don't think. A spiritual gift is a skill that the Spirit anoints to be effective. The effect is not always just conversion. It's the pricking of consciences. It's the deepening of love for the Lord. It's the correcting of behavior in others.

Here's what I tell young people at Bethlehem if they're trying to discern what the Lord wants them to do. I say, "Just start doing what you love to do. Pray down blessing on it, and see what people affirm. If you're in a small group, they're going to affirm that you're a helper and lover. They're going to affirm that you're an effective teacher or whatever." And so I presume that these missionaries had some experience where they did some ministry, and it blessed people. And then they had to believe God is for them, that he's going to use them, and then they go.

We should be thankful that those early missionaries didn't have airplanes because perhaps they would have come home early. If you have to get on a boat and ride for six months, you stick it out another year, and another year, and another year. That may be why today we don't have the same kinds of stories, because it's just so easy to bail now and it wasn't in those days.

When the Bible says elders must have evidence of spiritual faithfulness and be "able to teach" (Gk. *didaktios*; 1 Tim. 3:2), I don't think that just means he's good at what he does and nobody gets helped. I think the evidence of being apt to teach is that lights go on in people. They see things in the Word that they haven't seen before. Affections are changed, and others confirm that he has a gift.

That's what happened to me. First I taught seventh-grade boys at Lake Avenue Church in Pasadena, then ninth-grade boys, then the Galilean Sunday School class, then I assisted William LaSor in Greek at Fuller Theological Seminary. And the words started coming. "We understand you. We don't understand LaSor. You help us make sense of this." I started feeling like maybe that's who I am. My identity arose in community. You can't go into the woods and figure out who you are. It's totally ambiguous. So you stay in the church and you love people and you do what you love to do, and suddenly you start to discover who you are within the context of community.

Justin Taylor: When you personally get discouraged and want to throw in the towel, where do you go biblically? Is there a particular passage or book that you find yourself returning to over and over again? And where do you go outside the Bible? Is there a particular author or book that you return to over and over again when you're discouraged or downcast?

John MacArthur: I don't tend to be that way. I don't know why. I'm not really a melancholy type of person. I just move to the next responsibility. There's no time for me to sit and feel sorry or feel bad. There's too much to do. I mean, I'll sometimes get discouraged, but the next task looms large. People have no idea what it is to preach week after week after week after week, year after year, decade after decade to the same people, who have recorded everything you've ever said, and then to speak in chapel at a college and chapel at a seminary, and work on a book, and so on. For me, this is the track the Lord has put me on. There's no time. I don't have time to sit. If I have those kinds of moments, fleeting as they may be, I always think of the apostle Paul. Or I think of some of my personal heroes. My mind often goes to William Carey, when all of his manuscripts burned. Or it goes to William Tyndale (who is a particular treasure in my mind), who is sitting in prison about to die and wants somebody to bring him a needle and thread so he can sew up his leggings because he's cold. I've stood by Robert Morrison's grave and cried in China.

It's not a long process for me, because there's just a relentless schedule. I preach one message on Sunday morning, another message on Sunday night, and usually another time every week, somewhere else in one of our ministries. So I don't seem to have time to let those things get me down. When I prepare a message, to this day I am so infused with the thrill of what I've learned and the eagerness to preach it that it drags me past whatever might have discouraged me. And even when I preach a really dumb sermon and all I want to do is hide somewhere, the sooner I can start working on next week's sermon the better, because I will leave that behind and I will move into that new opportunity. For me it's just getting into the Word and digging in and discovering what I need to know for the next ministry.

John Piper: I probably pray the prayer "Keep me and preserve me" as often as I pray any prayer. I mean, "Keep me saved," because I think God uses means to cause us to persevere. I mean, "Keep me in the ministry." I don't want to be one of these short-lived people. I mean, "Keep me married." I don't want to wreck it that way. And I mean, "Keep me." I pray that. "Now to him who is able to keep you . . ." (Jude 24). I pray that blessing down on me a lot. And the Lord has spared me.

There is something to men in midlife crisis. I remember one time, I was forty, sitting on the steps halfway through vacation sobbing. Noël comes down the steps. "What's wrong?" I said, "I don't have a clue." It was like PMS. And I just said, "I don't know if I want to stay. I don't know if I want. . . . I don't have a clue why I'm so sad." And that season lasted several years, and the grace was that I could still function. I was listening to another author the other day. She was asked, "What's the best thing about writing?" And she said, "The last page." What's great about depression is the light at the end of the tunnel. Nobody enjoys being depressed in the middle of it.

But one more thing with regard to solutions. I have spent a lot of effort to develop a theology of suffering. This conference and book exist to answer that question. I want to last. I want to stay in. I want to get through the discouraging times. I want to help you not be fickle, wishy-washy, dropout, trade-your-life-away, swap-wives, leave-jobs, trade-churches kind of people. I just don't want you to be that way, so I created a conference (and now this book).

John MacArthur earlier recounted for us the endless sufferings of the apostle Paul.[3] So when you asked him about discouragement, he said, "I go to Paul." And I say, "Amen, me too." I look at 2 Corinthians 1:9: "We were so unbearably crushed to make us rely surely not on ourselves but on God who raises the dead." And I preach that to myself. Here I am feeling that way. *I feel like it would be so nice to go to heaven right now. Just let me go to heaven. Noël can take care of Talitha. It will all work out. Just let me go.* And at that moment, the answer comes back: "No. If your heart just keeps beating, then you have to do theology." I'm wired that way. I do theology. I say, "God struck Paul down in order that he might not rely on himself but on the God who raises the dead. He wanted him to be desperate. You're desperate, so he must have a purpose for you." And I just preach myself through a theology of suffering back into, I hope, more usefulness.

Keep on working on your "sovereignty of God" piece and your "evil of the world" piece. Those are the greatest issues in life. How can God be sovereign and there be so much horror in the world, including the horror in your own life that's making you so discouraged?

John MacArthur: I think it's not the things I feel. It's how that processes in me, as all of the spiritual battles, all of the disappointments, all the griefs, all the heartbreaks. I don't know. I'm wired to deal with those in a different way. I can't imagine just sitting and crying and not know why I was doing it. But that's not to say that I don't feel the same longings on the inside. It's how they get processed, I think. The

---

[3]See Chapter 3.

spiritual battle for me is the same as it is for anyone. At this point in my life, I feel that in many ways I'm here because I've escaped by the hair of my chinny-chin-chin. But there could have been a thousand points at which through my life it all would have been ashes. It's not to say that's not a reality or that I'm not aware of that. It's the way I deal with it that is different. I don't know why. It's just the way I'm wired.

Justin Taylor: How do you want to be remembered? What do you want people to say about you when you die? What do you want to be known for?

John MacArthur: John, do you ever think about that?

John Piper: Yes. Every funeral.

John MacArthur: I'm not trying to plan my post-death world.

John Piper: No, this is not a plan. You don't get to plan it. But you do get to think about it.

I would like them to say that I was humble, and I don't think they will. I'd like all my sons to say that I was a really tenderhearted, sensitive, understanding father. I think they'll say other things. I'd like my church to say that I was really there for them. And I don't think they'll say that.

So you might ask me, "Why aren't you changing your lifestyle?" And the answer is that I've tried. I've tried, and I'm still working at it. But if they say that I was a means to many people getting a passion for the supremacy of God in all things for the joy of all peoples through Jesus Christ, I'll be okay if that's on my tombstone. Paul said that what man says isn't going to count anyway (cf. Rom. 14:4). One person's verdict isn't going to matter. So whatever's written on my tombstone will be a small consequence compared to the Judge of the last day. And I think what he'll look for is evidence that I was cleaving to Christ for my righteousness and my punishment.

Justin Taylor: Would you please close us in prayer?

John Piper: Father in heaven, we feel a great need for you, and we love grace. We love mercy. We love the fact that our ministry is given by mercy, our salvation is given by mercy, our breath is given by mercy, our singleness is given by mercy, our marriage is given by mercy, and our children are given and taken by mercy. We are a people who eat and drink and sleep and breathe mercy. And this is the way we would have it be. You exalt yourself to show mercy. And we are happy to be the beneficiaries while you get the glory and you get the praise and you get the fame. We get the joy. Through Christ I pray. Amen.

Scripture Index

Subject Index

✖ desiringGod

If you would like to further explore the vision of God and life presented in this book, we at Desiring God would love to serve you. We have hundreds of resources to help you grow in your passion for Jesus Christ and help you spread that passion to others. At our website, desiringGod.org, you'll find almost everything John Piper has written and preached, including more than thirty books. We've made over twenty-five years of his sermons available free online for you to read, listen to, download, and in some cases watch.

In addition, you can access hundreds of articles, find out where John Piper is speaking, learn about our conferences, discover our God-centered children's curricula, and browse our online store. John Piper receives no royalties from the books he writes and no compensation from Desiring God. The funds are all reinvested into our gospel-spreading efforts. Desiring God also has a whatever-you-can-afford policy, designed for individuals with limited discretionary funds. If you'd like more information about this policy, please contact us at the address or phone number below. We exist to help you treasure Jesus Christ and his gospel above all things because he is most glorified in you when you are most satisfied in him. Let us know how we can serve you!

Desiring God
Post Office Box 2901 Minneapolis, Minnesota 55402
888.346.4700   mail@desiringGod.org